Soc

STRESS AND DEPRESSION IN CHILDREN AND TEENAGERS

VICKY MAUD, one of Britain's busiest agony aunts, works for many regional newspapers across the United Kingdom. She appears extensively on radio and television where she uses her training in counselling to help listeners and viewers. Vicky is the UK representative on the executive board of the International Centre for Drug Abuse Prevention in Schools and has travelled all over the world with this work. She has close links with Depression Alliance and has been a key speaker and counsellor at their conferences over the years. Married with four children, her interests include travel, reading, cooking, psychic interests, dream analysis and walking by the sea. She is the author of *How to Enjoy your Retirement* (Sheldon Press, 1996) and *Depression at Work* (Sheldon Press, 2000).

D0316405

Overcoming Common Problems Series

For a full list of titles please contact
Sheldon Press, Marylebone Road, London NW1 4DU

Overcoming Common Problems

Stress and Depression in Children and Teenagers

Vicky Maud

First published in Great Britain in 2002 by
Sheldon Press
1 Marylebone Road
London NW1 4DU

Copyright © Vicky Maud 2002

All rights reserved. No part of this book may be reproduced
or transmitted in any form or by any means
electronic or mechanical, including photocopying,
recording, or by any information storage and retrieval system,
without permission in writing from the publisher.

British Library Cataloguing-in-Publication Data
A catalogue record for this book is available from the British Library

ISBN 0–85969–857–2

Typeset by Deltatype Limited, Birkenhead, Merseyside
Printed in Great Britain by Biddles Ltd
www.biddles.co.uk

HOUNSLOW LIBRARIES	
FEL	
002295735	
Askews	16-Jun-2006
155.418	£6.99

Contents

With love to my children Philip, Louise, John and Lucy, who have given me so much happiness.

Acknowledgements

This has probably been the hardest of my books to write because I have had to take an honest look at how I brought up my children, and at my own childhood. Like most people, there are things that I would have changed and those that I am glad that I did. By the time this book is published I will have been married to Ken for 40 years. Like many people, we made mistakes and struggled at times to bring our children up, but somewhere along the line we must have done something right to have four lovely children who we are so proud of today. I want to thank both them and Ken for being there for me, especially when I was ill.

My grateful thanks go to Rosemary, who laboriously typed up my book, and to my solicitor Victoria Kenny, who saved the day by lending me her recording machine when mine decided to give up the ghost. Also, to my youngest daughter Lucy, who wrote about her experiences of being badly bullied, which I know was very difficult for her.

I would also like to say a big thank you to Michele Elliott at Kidscape, who has always been at the end of the phone if I needed advice, and also Depression Alliance, who I have worked with for many years and who have never stinted on their support.

Last but by no means least, I want to thank the readers of my columns who generously wrote in with their experiences, which has helped so much in writing this book.

Foreword

Dear Friend,

When we look back at our childhood most of us will do so through 'rose-coloured spectacles', and memories of holidays, family outings, being with friends, long summer holidays, first girlfriend or boyfriend, will all come flooding back. Unless we have endured bullying, family rows or intimidation, lesser times of unhappiness will fade into the distant past, leaving us feeling that our childhood was the happiest time of our life.

For some inexplicable reason, most people think their children will always be happy during their childhood, and the fact that they might become depressed is something that is often dismissed out of hand. Depression is associated in most people's minds with adults, and many find it very difficult to relate this problem to children, but the truth is that lots of our young people do suffer with both stress and depression. Most parents don't recognize the symptoms, and their children don't even know what depression is.

Statistics have shown that depression affects at least 2 in 100 children under the age of 12 and 5 in every 100 teenagers, which is very worrying indeed. In my broadcasting work as an agony aunt I answer problems that are e-mailed in from teenagers, children, parents and teachers. Added to this are the many letters that I receive on my newspaper columns from young people. Consequently, I have become increasingly worried at the suffering many of them are going through. Some contact me because they are being abused, others cannot cope with parental pressure to do well at school, and exams stress out yet more of them.

In addition, there are also the changes in lifestyle for youngsters because of parents splitting up, having to accept stepparents, and often being expected to take sides when parents argue. These are all causes of stress and depression in our children today.

Bullying has to come close to the top of the list of causes, with thousands of children across the country setting off for school each day, scared, unhappy and isolated. Many never tell their parents, or anyone else for that matter, what they are going through; they suffer day after day at the hand of their tormentors, scared to say anything for fear the bullying will get worse. Sadly, some commit suicide. How can all these dreadful things be happening to our children when we haven't even realized they are becoming stressed and depressed? Unfortunately the answer to that is easy: we are not expecting it, and are quick to find other reasons for our children's symptoms and behaviour.

What we might see as bad behaviour in our child may be their way of expressing the depressed feelings – in the same way that anger in an adolescent, or an extreme behaviour pattern, can. Depression and stress are also very clever at disguising themselves in a whole range of physical symptoms that can confuse the picture, or point to other illnesses instead.

I hope that this book will help parents, relatives, teachers and friends of youngsters who are depressed to recognize the symptoms, identify the causes, and help them back on the road to recovery, without making them feel guilty or uncomfortable about what is an illness just like any other.

Looking back on my own childhood, I would say that I could come up with enough happy times to fill a book, but if I am honest there were times when I felt very unhappy, not because my parents didn't love or care for me, but because of circumstances.

I was the eldest of two children, with a six-year gap between my younger brother and me. My mum suffered from agoraphobia, which meant she never left the house without my father. Dad worked long hours because we needed the money, and at the age of eight or nine I used to take the washing to the launderette each week, and do all the shopping when I came home from school. I didn't mind, and I wanted to help my mum, but sometimes when I saw my friends playing in the square outside our flat I had this little cloud that built up inside me, making me feel miserable that I was missing out on playing with my friends.

On Saturdays I had to do the 'big shop' because Dad was working, and this would mean at least three journeys to the local co-op. If I was lucky, I was allowed to go out to the Saturday morning pictures first, and then do the shopping at lunchtime. I didn't resent it because I knew no different, but I did feel weighed down by all the responsibility.

I longed for the school holidays when I would be sent to Bangor in north Wales, to spend the time with my grandmother. There I was free to play, to wander on the pier, and to paddle in the Ravendachi, a little brook that ran down to the beach. It is strange that I haven't wondered about this until I wrote it down – but who did all the shopping when I was in Wales?

As I got older, I went to the grammar school and things changed. I had a long bus journey to London each day, and would pick up a few items for my mum on the way home, but the 'big shop' stopped – I still don't know who did that. Responsibility partially lifted, I felt less stressed, but this was offset by the feelings of being very much on my own, and sad when it came to parental support at school. With Mum's agoraphobia and Dad working all the hours he could, neither of them ever came to school events. Medicals I endured alone, parents evenings were not attended, and I felt I must have been the only child in the school whose parents were never at prize-giving (not that I ever got one), or at the yearly service that was held in Southwark Cathedral.

I don't know if I suffered with depression or stress, but what I do know is that there were times when I felt very unhappy. Never more so, in fact, than when a man on a bike attacked me on my way home from school. I was on a very lonely lane, which I had to walk along to get to school every day. It was a footpath between a cemetery and an allotment. This path climbed a steep hill and turned at the top, and at this point you were about a quarter of a mile in either direction from the roads. Looking back and having visited the spot with my family since, I can't believe I was allowed to walk this way, as so few people used it. On this particular day I was with three or four friends on our way home when a man on his bike stopped and dropped his newspaper. 'Pick that up for me please,' he asked, and I did. Next thing I knew he had grabbed me and was doing things that I didn't understand. I wasn't raped. Fortunately, a lady came along and hit him with an umbrella, and he shot off down the hill, still on his bike. 'Run home and tell your mother what has happened,' she said.

Scared and embarrassed in front of my friends I tried to run, only to find I fell over because my knickers were around my ankles. When I got home, I told my mum what had happened and she went very quiet. She told me to get into the bath and then go to bed. Later I heard muffled voices as they discussed what had happened. They came and tucked me up, gave me a cuddle, and never ever mentioned it again. Not, I'm sure, because they didn't care, but because I honestly believe that they felt it was the best for me if it was all forgotten. For the next six months, I had to go to school and back along the same road. I would try to find reasons not to go to school. At school I would sit in class terrified at the thought of going home in case the man was waiting for me again. I used to lie in bed at night unable to sleep, scared and dreading the next day. Looking back, I think I was definitely depressed at that time. I don't think my parents knew how much this affected me, and how it has ever since. Even now, I'm wary when I'm going out alone. I never go to lonely places, and used to have nightmares that something similar might happen to either of my two lovely daughters.

My salvation was getting a place at a grammar school, which gave me choices. I chose a school in central London as I couldn't bear the thought of going to school near where I lived, and where I might bump into this man again. Soon after this we moved to a different area, and the sun seemed to come out for me again and the unhappy feelings drifted away. I couldn't tell my parents how I felt, because I didn't want to upset them. I loved them, and I knew they loved me. Our Christmases were magical, birthday parties special, they made my friends welcome, and the flat where we lived was a happy place to come home to. I had so much to thank them for that these unhappy feelings I kept to myself didn't seem to matter too much. Maybe I displayed anger or was moody – I can't remember, but I certainly know that it is possible to live in the most loving home and to still get depressed as a child.

If you have picked this book up, you are either a parent with an open mind, or one who is concerned about their child or teenager. Whether you read this book from cover to cover, or just dip into particular sections, doesn't matter. Because the book covers quite a wide age range (between 5 and 19 in some parts), it has often been necessary to use the words 'child' or 'children' to encompass all age groups. I have tried to cover as much as I can in a sensitive and honest way. Some of the case histories may bring tears to your eyes, but as you brush them away you will know that you will be able to help your child should the need arise.

Kind regards,
Vicky

1

Could my child be depressed?

Dymphna sat in her office feeling stunned, hurt and angry. How dare her colleagues say she was a misery and never laughed or smiled. She could share a laugh and a joke with anyone when she was in the right frame of mind. Just because she didn't walk around with a stupid grin on her face all day, this didn't give them the right to make nasty remarks.

At 29, Dymphna had been at the bank for seven months and thought she got on well with most of the staff. A few weeks earlier there had been a retirement party for one of the women, and a group photograph was taken which was to be submitted to the editor of the staff magazine that came out every quarter.

It was this that prompted the comment that she had spoilt the photo by looking 'as miserable as sin'. The situation was not helped when someone else added 'as usual'.

That night, Dymphna sat and thought about what had been said. It wasn't the first time people had described her as a misery or commented that she had a face as long as a fiddle. Dymphna had been diagnosed with depression four years earlier, and during counselling she had talked about the sad, heavy feeling that had hung over her since childhood.

'Do I really look miserable?' she asked herself. 'Have I always done so?' She thought back to all the times that her parents had taken family photographs when she was a child, and how she was constantly being told to smile. Only later that night, when she was looking through an old photo album, did she realize that there were no photos of her laughing or smiling or showing happiness. Instead, there were only photos with a false smile or a sad stare.

No one had suggested that she had been depressed since her childhood, but now Dymphna found herself wondering if she had been. But surely this couldn't be possible – 'children don't suffer with depression', she told herself.

Sadly, they do. There are many misconceptions about children and depression, with one of the most common responses to hearing that a child is depressed being, 'What have they got to be depressed about?' or, 'They have no worries – everything is done for them.'

Others come out with stupid statements such as, 'They're just

1

spoilt!' or, 'They don't know when they are well off!' or, 'They haven't got enough to occupy their minds!' All these sayings show a total lack of understanding about depression.

The death of a loved one, parents divorcing, being abandoned, physical or mental abuse, can all trigger depression. However, some children become depressed long before any of these trigger factors can affect them. Therefore, we have to accept that depression can be caused totally by a chemical imbalance in the brain, wholly by psychological factors, or by a combination of both.

As with adults, a diagnosis of depression in children is not as clear-cut as it is for other illnesses. Unlike many other ailments, there is no test that can positively say that someone is depressed or pinpoint the causes. What we can do is be aware that some children are at risk, and thus more predisposed to depression than others.

Helping anxious toddlers and young children

Let us now look at some of the behaviour patterns of young children and try to unravel what is part of normal growing up and what could be stress-related and lead on to depressed feelings.

In very young children, physical reasons such as tiredness, hunger or feeling unwell can make them irritable and upset, and are not usually stress-related. When they become toddlers, they can become clingy and anxious because they are very sensitive or timid. Sometimes it is because they find new situations more difficult to cope with than other children do.

Although many grow out of this phase, some children don't – they feel unable to mix with others and get very distressed when separated from their mother or have to sleep alone. Here are some ways in which we can help anxious toddlers and young children:

- By not arguing in front of them.
- Not confusing them with too many choices, even though it is good for them to make some decisions as they get older.
- Giving them the safety of boundaries and the knowledge that we are there to protect them.
- When there are family rows or illness, remembering that children worry and often blame themselves. We need to give reassurance that everything will be all right and that it is not their fault.
- Remembering that death frightens children, and that they will need help if someone they love dies.

2

- Not using excessive threats – these only burden children and make them even more anxious.
- Not taking away a child's comfort toy or security blanket, because this often helps them to cope.
- Not seeking reassurance all the time from our children; this will only burden them.
- Giving them lots of different experiences – for example, visiting places, meeting people, and playing with other children.
- Frightening experiences can bring special fears. If you feel this applies to your child, talk to them and seek help through your doctor.
- When old enough, encouraging our children to write stories about how they feel, or to draw a picture.
- Being aware that if there is a new baby in the family, this may cause anxiety in our children.

Helping teenagers deal with stress

Teenagers' physical and mental health can deteriorate very much if there are family problems – for example, if a parent becomes unemployed or there is a divorce. Even parents who never intend to split up will argue, and do not realize the damage they could be doing to their offspring. While they are shouting they are unaware that their children and teenagers may be crying in their bedrooms, or trying to shut out the argument by covering their ears or turning up their music. Some even leave the house. So, it's important that we think before we argue!

Hormonal changes are normal and account for a lot of moodiness and restless feelings in teenagers. What *we* know to be normal can often be frightening for them, especially as they may be developing at a different rate to their friends, and don't want to appear different. We need to get the balance right by understanding that their friends are playing a larger part in their lives now. But we still have to provide stable, caring homes for them – without appearing to be over-protective or 'going on at them' all the time.

Most teenagers will seek excitement and take risks at times. In the majority of cases they come through OK with no emotional scars, but for some it leads on to behaviour that gets them into trouble and leads to them becoming emotionally disturbed.

Here are some ways that you can help your teenager:

- You can help by listening and talking honestly about what you did as a teenager. They may be surprised how like you they are.

3

- Talk to your partner and make sure that you both give the same messages to your teenager. (Obviously this may not apply if you are a single parent.)
- Discuss and set clear and sensible ground rules.
- Have a 'bargaining and compromise session' each week. This means that they agree to do something you want, or that will make things easier in the family, and you do the same for them.
- Try to be understanding – think back to when you were a teenager and some of the problems you had, and how difficult it might have been for you.

Stepfamilies

Whatever the age of your children, if you have a stepfamily situation you may be experiencing difficulties. It will take time for them to accept that their mum or dad has a new partner and also that they may have to live with stepsisters and stepbrothers. Your children wanted things to go on as they were – not to change. So try not to expect too much of your children – or your partner. Never try to turn them against their other parent, or stop them seeing one another. Likewise, it is not helpful to criticize the relationship your stepchildren have with your partner, or he or she has with your children. If you need help on any parenting issues, including stepfamilies, you can phone ParentlinePlus (0808 800 2222) or if you have access to the internet visit their website (www.parentlineplus.co.uk).

If you specifically want to talk to someone about stepfamilies, you can telephone Stepfamily Scotland who are willing to take calls from anyone in the United Kingdom on 0131 225 5800, or you can visit their website (www.stepfamilyscotland.org.uk).

The stigma of depression

Sadly, there is still a lot of stigma attached to depression, and people tend to urge you to 'pull yourself together' because they do not understand it, or are frightened of anything to do with a mental illness. Parents often mistakenly label a depressed child as moody, difficult or sullen, leaving them feeling that it is all their fault and that they are bad. Instead of youngsters getting the help they need, things are made worse because they are chastised for behaviour that they have no control over.

Whatever the reason for you picking up this book, your mind is open to understanding what may be troubling your child. It may not be easy, but if you can recognize depression in your unhappy child, you will be in a position to help them overcome it. Apart from getting your child professional help, though, there are things that parents can do to help.

Relaxation

Relaxation is an excellent way of easing tension and brushing away sad feelings, and you could try the following exercises with your child. Depending on their age, you can adapt the exercises to make them fun. For instance, when doing the relaxation of the body exercises with very young children, get them to imagine that they are a favourite animal or cartoon character, and make it into a game.

Bedtime relaxation game for young children
Let your child choose which animal or cartoon character they want to be, and then say that you are going to help them to go to sleep. You can pretend to be an animal as well if you want to, and both make animal noises to make it more fun. Find a CD or cassette of some gentle soft music, maybe from one of their favourite films such as *The Lion King* or *Jungle Book*, and have this playing softly in the background.

1 Get them to lie comfortably and close their eyes.
2 Explain that they have had a very hard day (either in the jungle or whatever is relevant to the animal or character that they have chosen), but now it is bedtime. However, say that before they go to sleep they need to do some exercises that will make them feel nicely relaxed, sleepy, and will keep them safe in the night.
3 Get them to tighten up (squeeze) all the muscles in their feet, and then relax them.
4 Using the same tightening and relaxing techniques, get them to do the same with their right leg, then their left, and then both together.
5 Then continue up the body, asking them to tighten up the muscles in their bottom, tummy, chest, back, shoulders, hands, arms, neck, and finally their face – then relaxing them.
6 Now tell them to listen to the music and think nice thoughts until they drift off to sleep.

Relaxation for teenagers

For teenagers, relaxation should also be done near bedtime – again with soft music in the background. The methods given here cover relaxation of the mind as well as the body:

Relaxation of the body and mind

Relaxation of the body

1 Sit or lie comfortably.
2 Close your eyes gently. Become aware of your body and how it feels.
3 Concentrate on your breathing – slow and gentle.
4 Tighten the muscles in your feet. Be aware of how it feels. Slowly let the tension go. Let your feet feel heavy and relaxed.
5 Using this technique of tightening and relaxing, continue up the body. Tighten and relax your calf and thigh muscles. Repeat for the other leg. Then use the method on buttocks, abdomen, back, chest, shoulders, hands, lower and upper arms, neck, and finally your face.
6 When your whole body is relaxed, become aware of your breathing again. Relax the whole body further. Lie quietly for several minutes.
7 When you are ready, slowly bring your body back to a state of readiness. Open your eyes while still lying down. Do not sit up until you are quite ready.

Relaxation of the mind

1 Sit or lie comfortably.
2 Close your eyes.
3 Relax all your muscles (as in the relaxation of the body exercise) from feet to face.
4 Breathe through your nose and listen to your breathing.
5 Repeat the word 'one' or any other sound you choose for this purpose and relax still further.
6 Continue for 10–20 minutes. Do not use an alarm. You will soon learn to judge the time naturally. At the end, let yourself become gradually aware of your surroundings. Sit or lie quietly for a while before standing up.

During relaxation time, do not try to force yourself to be relaxed. This will come naturally. Let any distracting thoughts flow through your mind rather than trying to banish them. Gently bring your word or thought back into focus. Practising when you go to bed should help you to sleep once you have got into the routine of it. It should not be done too soon after a heavy meal.

The beauty of these exercises is that they can also help parents relax at a time when they are worried about their children.

Visualization

Another way to help your children is to encourage them to do visualization. This is probably easier for older children and teenagers, but – if kept simple – it can work for younger children as well. The basis of visualization is to help them to relax, to give a feeling of well-being, and to feel in control.

'A gentle journey'

Once again, have soft gentle music playing in the background, but this time it should not have a theme that will detract the child or teenager from being able to focus on the visualization.

Teenagers can do this on their own, but children will need you to talk them through a visualization:

1 Get your child to lie down, close their eyes, and listen to the music.
2 Ask them to imagine that they are somewhere really nice, in a field, on the beach, or anywhere that they feel happy. Tell them that the sun is shining and they feel nice and warm. If they are on a beach, suggest that they let the sand trickle through their fingers, examine the pebbles, listen to the sea. If they are in a garden or a field, suggest that they can hear the birds singing, the leaves rustling, and can look at all the shapes and colours of the plants. Keep your voice soft and gentle and don't talk too much; give them time to see what they want to see.

Often children will drift off to sleep, and this doesn't matter. If they don't fall asleep, bring the visualization to a close after ten minutes or so. Do this gently by saying, 'It is time to leave your lovely beach [or wherever they are] now. Open your eyes and give me a smile.' Don't let them sit up too quickly; it is best to lie beside them and chat quietly for a few moments.

'The healing pool'

One visualization that helps teenagers and adults alike is centred on a pool, set in a beautiful garden, with marble steps leading down to it. The pool can be filled with warm or cool blue water, or a blue light. It doesn't matter which – the important thing is that they imagine that it will heal them and that they get a feeling of well-being. In the visualization, the person walks down the steps into the pool and absorbs the healing. They then walk out of the pool and wrap themselves in warm towels, which are laid on a table in the sun at the top of the steps. Hopefully this warmth will give them an even greater feeling of well-being.

'Your secret room'

When depression strikes older children and teenagers, it often feels as if their heads are bursting with worries and there is no way of getting these feelings out. No escape, no solitude, no peace or quiet.

Many years ago, a close friend of mine, Nerrys, told me what she thought was a good way of overcoming this. She explained that everyone needs their own space where they can go in their heads to be alone, and to work out ways of coping. So here is how you, or your teenager, can do it. (I will use the term 'you' throughout this exercise, but it will relate to either you, your child, or your teenager.)

1 Imagine a corridor or a house with many doors in it.
2 Choose a door – only you have the key to it.
3 Open the door and go into the room. The room can be any size or shape, and decorated as you want it, but it is empty apart from one shelf on a wall and a small wooden box on the floor with a pen and paper next to it.
4 It is up to you to put any furniture into this room in your mind – that is, if you want to. You can move the box anywhere in the room as well.
5 The purpose of the shelf is to put bottles, jars or containers on it. These can be any shape or size, or decorated in any way you want. In each of these there will be liquid or sweets that will help you feel better. So, for instance, you could have one labelled 'I Feel Sad', another 'Help Me Sort My Problems Out', or 'I Want To Be Understood', or 'Help Me To Talk To My Parents'. You can add as many containers as you like, and each time you go into the room, you can imagine that you take what you need and eat or drink it to help you feel better.
6 The box is there for your worries. When you have a worry, imagine that you are writing it on a piece of paper. Look at what you have written. If it is something that you know you can do something about, place it in the box and be determined to do this. If not, place it in the box and tell yourself that you are not going to get into a

state over it. Then put the lid firmly back on the box. You can always take the problem out of the box at a later time and deal with it then. Putting it away like this helps us to accept what we cannot change and to do something about what we can change.

7 This is your room for ever. No one else can visit it. You can change it as often as you want. It is your special place and one where you can help yourself.

The difficulties of being a parent

It is not easy being a parent, and we all come to it unprepared. Most of the time we muddle through, cope, or do well, but sometimes circumstances mean that we need help. Never be afraid or put off seeking help for yourself or your child. There are professionals out there who can help. They won't stick labels on your children, or lay the blame at your feet. They have the expertise to help you through difficult periods, so make sure that you get the support that you need. It is not a sign of weakness; it is the most sensible and caring thing that you can do.

Questions and answers

Here are some questions that have come in my mailbag and may strike a few chords:

Q I thought that I was very close to my 14-year-old daughter, but recently she has become very withdrawn and unhappy, and won't tell me what is wrong. I have now heard from the school that she has been stealing and lying. They want her to see a child psychologist, but have also asked whether there are any problems at home. Things are not good between my husband and I, and we have been talking about divorce. However, I feel that this is private and personal to us and no concern of the school. Should I allow her to see the child psychologist?

A Yes, provided your daughter is agreeable. You must not force her. Your daughter's behaviour has changed, and she needs help. The stealing could be her way of trying to get attention, or hitting back at the unhappy feelings she has inside. I know it will be hard to tell the school about your problems, but if you want to help your daughter, you should do so. They need to know what might be troubling her. Counselling can often be arranged for the whole family. Ask about this through your doctor and the school. This might make it seem more like a shared problem to your daughter, but if she prefers to see the school psychologist and talk alone, then don't feel excluded by this. It is what is best for her that counts.

Q My three-year-old cries a lot, gets into tempers, and then goes all clingy with me. I worry that he may be depressed because his grandfather has suffered with depression all his life, and says he can remember feeling miserable as a young child. What do you think?
A It sounds to me like 'terrible tantrum threes', and that with love and reassurance from you it will hopefully soon pass. However, with a family history of depression, it is always best to be watchful and seek advice from your health visitor or doctor. Be careful not to project your worries on to your son, otherwise you could make him anxious when there is no need.

Q I am a lad of 18 in my first term at university. I was looking forward to it, but now I am feeling depressed and lonely. I live in the halls of residence, but I don't have anything in common with the others, who are much more outgoing than me. I miss my family and home, and find the lectures and looking after myself very stressful. I spend every evening writing up notes, and then I cannot sleep, which means that I feel dreadful the next day. I am thinking of packing it in, but I know that my parents will be upset and disappointed if I do.
A Don't give up, for your own sake, otherwise you will regret a missed opportunity in the future. Although it is exciting going to university, it can be very stressful and a source of great anxiety. There are many practical things to sort out, such as money and food, but you will get used to this. It is natural to miss your family and home, but there are hundreds of other students there who, though they may not show it, feel the same as you do. I think that it is time to lighten up on yourself. You cannot burn the midnight oil all the time. Spend an hour on those notes and then go out with others to the Student Union or join a couple of campus clubs. You may not be the most outgoing of the lads, but you must learn to enjoy yourself and not shut yourself away.

2
School life and depression

At least a quarter of our children's day is spent at achool, away from the security of their home and family. Many of them find the pressures within school too much to cope with.

We bandy around the old saying 'schooldays are the happiest days of our life', but a lot of children and teenagers wouldn't agree. The pitfalls lie not only in having to absorb a vast quantity of knowledge, but also having to forge friendships, cope with peer pressure, falling out with friends, and often bullying as well. Added to this there are the pressures of homework, projects, exams and learning difficulties. It is little wonder that teenagers find themselves unable to cope.

With high class numbers, and staff stretched to their absolute capacity, often those who are experiencing difficulties go unnoticed. This is partly because there are so many other children, especially at secondary-school level, and also because children are very good at keeping their problems bottled up, and not bothering anybody with them. What should be a happy time of their lives is, for many, a nightmare.

Peer pressure at school

Peer pressure is one of the hardest things to cope with, and this can start from an early age in primary school. There always seems to be this need to conform – whether it be the way you dress, who your friends are, or the way you behave. In every class or year group, there appears to be a strong core of three or four boys or girls who seem to be able to set the rules for everyone else. They are usually the most vocal and confident, and often full of their own importance – they are probably used to getting their own way at home. They enforce what they see as the norm or the 'in-thing', and others – who may be scared of them – follow suit.

As parents, we have probably all done the 'shoe shop trail'. I know I have countless times, to the wails of, 'Mum, I *can't* wear those shoes, the other girls will make my life a misery if I do.' Yes, we are talking about shoes and peer pressure, not a world catastrophe. Even this can cause tears, and we haven't even reached the length of her skirt yet! 'Should her shirt really be hanging out in that untidy manner?' we ask ourselves as we hear for the hundredth time '*no one* wears a coat to school, Mum' as you watch them disappear down the road, shivering in a blazer! This may all seem very trivial, but to our youngsters it isn't. Peer pressure to have designer-label trainers, sports bags or jackets can be so great that it makes them depressed by worrying about it.

At primary school, peer pressure can be about what you wear, who you play with, and escalate to downright bullying. It is important to note any change in your child's behaviour, particularly who they talk about and play with. If you notice they are not playing with a particular friend, or stop asking if they can bring them back for tea, be aware, even if you don't say anything, that there may be a shift in this friendship and they could have fallen out. Often children put a lot of pressure on one another. I say this because not all of our children are the ones that suffer from peer pressures – there are some that *instigate* it. We must never think that our children, however much we love them, are perfect. Also, peer pressure at primary-school level is often a result of misunderstandings, not malice.

I once had a very distressing phone call from a mother of one of my daughter's best friends. Having recently been widowed, she was finding it hard to cope, and so were her children. On this particular day her daughter had come home from school sobbing because my daughter had been asking her questions about her father's death. At the time they were both seven. Understanding that the mother was angry, as she had enough on her plate without her daughter being pressurized in any way, I was horrified to think that my daughter could have caused this upset. When I spoke to my daughter it all became clear. She didn't understand death – it frightened her. She thought her friend would be able to explain things, as her dad had died two weeks before. Two hours later (with lots of tears from all four of us) we were sitting in this lady's house, apologies had been made, she had understood what had happened, and we still remain friends.

In this instance, the mother came direct to me as she knew me well, but if you feel your child is suffering from peer pressure, you have every right to go to the school and ask for it to be sorted out. The same goes for bullying, which I shall deal with in greater depth in a later chapter.

In secondary school, the pace of peer pressure is accelerated so much that one wonders how they even have time to fit in school work. The most sensitive ones go to the wall. These poor souls are the ones whose lives are made a misery and become susceptible to depression.

We have talked about peer pressure concerning appearances and clothes, but more serious problems arise when we get into the area of how teenagers behave. Take, for instance, the story of Keith, a nice young lad of 14, happy at home, and just wanting to go to school with no hassle:

Unfortunately for Keith his peer group had other ideas, and asked him if he wanted to be in their gang. At first he refused but then changed his mind, because he felt safer being one of them, rather than a victim of their bullying. One of the things the gang did was steal on the way home from school. Their target was the local sweet shop or, if they felt very brave, the CDs from Woolworths. They told Keith he had to steal, or things would be worse for him. He didn't want to do it, but he was totally out of his depth. One day he felt a hand on his shoulder as he left Woolworths and his world fell apart. His so-called mates were long gone, having got wind that Keith had been rumbled. Keith was taken off to the manager's office, while his parents were called. It was a nightmare, and he was violently sick even before his parents arrived. Keith got a caution and he is not allowed to go near the store again. The gang saw him as a bit of a hero, especially as he hadn't 'grassed on them'. He was warned about distancing himself from the group, which they didn't like, but fortunately they haven't given him too much hassle and he has made other friends.

Peer pressure regarding sex or drugs

Peer pressure to sleep with a boyfriend or girlfriend is a problem for teenagers today. Everyone else says they are having sex, so the pressure is on others to do the same. It is because of this that many girls and boys are losing their virginity far too soon, to partners who mean very little to them. Some girls get pregnant the very first time they have sex, because they were not prepared for it to happen. They didn't like to say no for fear of what their friends might say.

One of the worst times for peer pressure is when drugs are involved. 'Just try it', they will say, 'Don't be a wuss – it will make you feel great . . .' Sadly, far too many teenagers give in because they don't want to be seen to be different. If your child or teenager is a victim of peer pressure, try to talk to them about the effect it is having on them and how it can be overcome. Explain that it is easy to follow the pack, but sometimes you have to be yourself, and an individual, to avoid getting into trouble. Like bullying, it is something the schools are aware of, and they can do something about it. Don't ever feel that your child has to put up with peer pressure or bullying.

Making friends at school

As I said earlier in this chapter, one of the important things at school is to have friends, and ones that you can trust. Youngsters need friends who are there for them when they get into trouble at school, feel down about relationships, or things seem bad at home. Break-time is like an oasis in the desert, when they can chat with their friends and forget lessons for a short time.

Sadly, there are always some children who fail to make friends, often because of their own shyness. For parents this can be very worrying. If your child seems to be rejected or disliked by their peer group, it could be caused by one of two things: either their peers are a nasty bunch who are not worth worrying about, or your child doesn't have a lot in common with them.

Teenagers can often be rejected by their peers because they are quiet and withdrawn, offer no opinions, and don't try to get involved in activities or discussions. Others may be seen as aggressive, pushy or annoying to talk to, because they interrupt a lot and don't know how to listen. Both can be overcome, and you can help them to do it. Gently encourage them to be aware of their behaviour towards others, explain that it is important to be a good listener, and to show a sense of humour, to be trustworthy, and to share. Try to check that they never put down or insult others, talk behind classmates' backs, or betray confidences.

If your child has a problem with their peer group accepting them, get them to look in the mirror and ask them what they see. Make them feel good about themselves by telling them their strong points. Sometimes we try to be someone we are not, or put up barriers because we are scared of being rejected or seen as being unfriendly. Explain it is important they see the real person, and that you don't have to change into someone else – and also, to remember that it is not what you look like that matters, but the person inside that counts.

Encouragement to try to fit in, and to get involved, will pay off – as will trying to start conversations rather than always waiting for someone else to talk to them. Discuss what clubs or activities there are within school and outside that they would like to be part of, and where they could make friends. Encourage them to say nice things to others when they do well and, above all, to keep smiling and be on the look-out for those who may also be in need of a friend.

Falling out with friends at school

If your child comes home from school or college having fallen out with a friend, they will probably feel angry, hurt and isolated. These are all perfectly normal feelings, and ones that can be overcome. From your child's point of view, the best way to defuse the anger is to talk about it. So try to stop whatever you are doing and make time for them. If possible, now – not later! Suggest that they talk to another friend, as the more they talk the easier it will be to look at what has happened and decide what to do next. Youngsters' tactics usually range from totally ignoring the offending person, or giving them the benefit of a torrent of abuse the next time they meet up; however, neither tactic is effective – and nor is trying to drum up support from others in their group to gang up on the 'offender'.

Here are some points that you may want to pass on to your youngsters. Suggest a cooling-off period – even if first they rant, rage and bash a few cushions to get rid of angry feelings. Then help them to make up their minds about the best way to solve this problem, no matter whose fault it is. Explain that it is best to talk to the person they have fallen out with and to try not to argue. Make suggestions:

- Finding a solution is far better than just blaming the other person. After all, how many friends do either of you have that you can afford to lose one over an argument?
- It is miserable being at loggerheads, so try to stay cool.
- When there is an argument, sometimes it is best to walk away rather than to say something you may regret.
- Listen to what the other person is saying and try not to interrupt.
- Show respect for the other person's opinion, even if you don't agree with it, and don't pass judgement.
- Try to come up with a solution that you can both be happy with.

Falling out with friends can easily lead to depressed feelings, especially if the rift is not mended. Sometimes a little help from parents or teachers is all that is needed for the youngsters to become friends again.

Fourteen-year-old Lisa fell out with her best friend Claire because she had broken her promise and told some of the others in her class that Lisa's dad was in prison. Claire said, 'It just slipped out.' Lisa felt betrayed, and the focus of stares and whispers wherever she went. The row that broke out could be heard from one end of the school to the other. When confronted by staff, neither of them would say what they were arguing about. Both ended up in detention, and neither spoke to each other after that.

When Lisa got home, she was so angry that she hit her younger brother, who just happened to get in her way. He went running to his mum who had a real go at Lisa, making her misery even worse. She never told her mum what the problem was, and her mum never asked.

Up until this time, Lisa had been a model pupil, hard-working, never late, homework in on time, average marks. Gradually she slipped back, no one ever said anything to her about her dad, but she was convinced that nobody wanted anything to do with her any more. As for Claire, she was too scared of Lisa's present frame of mind to do anything other than stay out of her way.

Shoddy work, homework undone, and truancy now became Lisa's way of life. Teachers tried talking to her, but she stubbornly refused to talk. Her mother, unaware of this situation, was called into the school, but threw no light on to why Lisa had changed. She tried talking to Lisa, but Lisa locked herself in her room.

The occasional day off became more and more days when she wouldn't go to school. She became irritable, confused, wasn't eating, and lost interest in everything. She would sit for hours on end not saying a word, and crying herself to sleep at night.

It was her dad that Lisa confided in. Although she didn't realize it, she was telling him it was all his fault. If he hadn't stolen the money from his employer, none of this would have happened. He took this on board and helped her a lot over the coming months. Then one day, her mum noticed cuts on Lisa's arm and asked her how she had done them. 'I knocked my arm against a wall,' she lied. 'No you didn't,' piped up her young brother. 'I saw you digging your arm with your compass.' Lisa was depressed and self-harming. Her mother called the doctor, and this was the beginning of a long haul to restore her knocked confidence, lift her depression, and get back to school.

During this time her dad, who had been in an open prison for fraud, was released. He managed to get work, and family life improved a lot over the coming months. When she went back to school, no one mentioned her dad – except Claire, who apologized, and said the reason she told the others was because her parents were giving her grief over her friendship with Lisa because her dad was in prison. Claire couldn't cope and had confided in the others. Although there was no animosity between them, Lisa never trusted Claire again, and the friendship never recovered.

This was a tragic tale of how one mistake and a broken friendship led to depression for this 14-year-old girl.

Conflict with teachers

I think most of us have had children who come home from school saying there is a teacher who they can't get on with, they hate, or they feel doesn't like them. I know mine did. In most cases it passes, or they put up with it, but for some it can cause them to be very unhappy. If this happens with your child, take it seriously, and find out from the year head or head teacher what is going on, and do something about it.

Mark was a disruptive 13-year-old who met his match when a new PE master came to the school and was also his form teacher. Up until then, Mark had ruled the roost. Others looked up to him and joined in the antics that he created in classes taken by less strong members of staff. To maintain control when Mark was in the class was difficult – to say the least. When his parents chided him about his behaviour he would complain bitterly that the staff 'had it in for him'.

The new teacher, on the other hand, wasn't standing for any nonsense from Mark, and within days had respect from the rest of the class, leaving Mark to play up on his own. One day he took Mark aside and suggested that he channel his aggression and energies into sport. Mark was a keen footballer and, with his teacher's encouragement, he managed to get a place in the second team. From then on, Mark had a different attitude to school. A different approach might have had devastating results for Mark, but his teacher saw a problem and sensitively dealt with it.

Paul, on the other hand, following his brother, Lee, into the same school four years later, found that virtually every teacher was on their guard, expecting him to be as badly behaved as his brother, who had now left. Some teachers actually warned Paul that they would not stand for any nonsense, when he hadn't even put a foot wrong. Feeling very isolated, he found it hard to make friends, because the others gave him a wide berth as word had got around that he was trouble. Paul's brother Lee had been suspended three times before finally being expelled, and Paul was being pre-judged by everyone because of this. It was hard at 11 to put up a brave fight against the odds, even though he was well behaved. Paul's parents were not interested in what was going on at school, and he was left to cope alone. Quietly he got on with school life, and gradually the teachers relaxed. But he never did well, because he became very depressed; he left school with poor results.

In all walks of life there are people who don't get on, and it is no different at school. Occasionally it can be a conflict of personality between pupil and teacher and, if this occurs, changes should be made so it doesn't affect the pupil's education. If this happens with your child, ask for a meeting with the teacher concerned. Go with an open mind and be prepared to listen – and then put your child's side of the story, or ask if he or she can do it themselves. Remember this is your child, and you have every right to be concerned if you think there are problems with a member of staff.

Homework and exams

Homework and exams put major pressure on youngsters, so much so that they may become depressed. It is no easy task to come home from school and have to start work again. If adults had to do the same, I doubt most of us would find it easy.

If your child seems to find it difficult to cope with their homework and is getting upset and stressed, then do something about it. That is what the 'homework diary' is for. You probably sign it each week to say the homework is completed, but you have every right to say your child should stop at the end of the allotted time for that subject and put a note in the diary saying he or she couldn't finish within the time. No one expects children to be working each evening until midnight to complete subjects. Unless the teacher is told the amount that can be done by your child in the set time, they won't know if they are setting too much homework or if your child needs extra help. Whatever you do, don't become a 'homework parent' by doing most of the work yourself. Yes, you may achieve a good mark, but the pressure to do as well in class can make your child sick with worry.

Exams are the biggest stress time, especially at GCSE and at A level. Don't put pressure on your child to succeed. Help them arrange their revision and make sure there is plenty of time for relaxation as well. They can only do their best. Better a lower grade and to be happy than a high grade and for them to have to take antidepressants.

Truancy and school phobia

One of the signs that things have definitely taken a downward slide is when truancy occurs. Sometimes it can be a one-off because they felt fed up or haven't handed in some work, but if it occurs often, then you need to liaise very carefully with the school and, if necessary, ask if your child can see a school therapist or a counsellor to help them express their feelings.

If you have had a child who says he or she doesn't want to go to school, you will know just how difficult it can be to ascertain exactly what the problem is and how to deal with it.

Sometimes it will be because they have fallen out with friends, they don't get on with a certain teacher, or find a particular subject difficult to cope with. Just like adults, children can have days when they feel tired or under the weather and can't face going to school. These are all perfectly normal occurrences and, with understanding and a bit of gentle persuasion, the problem can usually be overcome.

There are, however, a number of children who dislike school intensely and avoid it as much as possible. These children are usually suffering with school phobia. Although statistics vary a lot on school phobia, it is estimated that the number of children who try to avoid going to school is over 5 per cent, but that those who are termed 'school phobic' is around 1 per cent or less. It is sometimes referred to as 'school refusing'.

Over half of those termed school phobic are boys, with the onset in most cases being between the ages of 11 and 12. This is understandable because it is a time when children go from primary to secondary school and are faced with many large changes in their lives.

There are some children who have problems between the ages of five and seven, and this can be caused by separation from their mothers, or worries about their home life. A few years ago I counselled a couple who were at loggerheads, but wanted to save their marriage. Although they didn't have big arguments, there were often raised voices with each one trying to score points over the other. They told me that their youngest child, aged seven, had started refusing to go to school when previously she had appeared to enjoy it. It was three months since they had managed to get her to go.

I suggested that they should talk to her about what was going on, in case she was only hearing snippets of conversations and was scared that one of them could disappear while she was at school. They did this, and found she was worried that they were going to divorce just as her friend's parents had. With reassurance, the following week she went back to school for a day, and within a month she was attending full time.

Children in their teens, particularly around the ages 13–15, who may be depressed can also become school refusers. It is important that depression is recognized and that help is sought. If your child becomes withdrawn, agitated, tearful, anxious, won't eat, or sleeps too much or too little, these could all indicate depression.

Sometimes refusing to go to school begins suddenly. This might be after a long absence from school due to illness, after school holidays, or a change of school or class. Although the event that triggered it off may seem to be the problem, it is more often the 'last stamp on the card' syndrome, where other things have built up beforehand.

In other cases, school refusing develops slowly. The occasional day becomes several days, then weeks, with visible signs of anxiety growing if pressure is put on them to go to school. Many children deny they are scared, but the signs may be obvious to parents – such as trembling or needing to pass urine frequently.

So what symptoms do children present as an excuse for staying away from school? Quite often a child will complain of pain, stomach problems or nausea in the morning, with these symptoms disappearing once the child is allowed to stay at home, but which reappear when he or she is pressurized into going to school.

Some children refuse point blank to go to school, offering no reason, while others will complain about fears that are associated with school, such as having to undress in front of others, feeling inadequate compared to friends, not being liked, bullied, or feeling unsafe when away from home.

School phobia should not be confused with truancy. Truants do not express or show any of the anxiety symptoms that I have mentioned.

If you feel your child could be suffering from school phobia, don't feel guilty. It is *not* your fault. Seek help through your doctor and the school, who may arrange for your child to see a child psychologist. It isn't easy to get a school refuser back to a normal school life, but with professional guidance it could be the first step towards relieving their anxieties and doing so.

I hope that this chapter has helped you to understand better the stresses and strains that your child might be under at school. There are problem areas that parents need to be able to think about, and in doing so they are in the best possible position to make sure that schooldays are as happy for their children as possible.

Questions and answers

Q My normal happy seven-year-old daughter has started making excuses for not going to school. She complains of feeling sick or tummy aches, but if I let her stay at home she is perfectly all right by mid-morning. If I make her go to school, I often get a phone call saying that she feels sick and would I collect her. Her teacher suggested that I took her to the doctor. He cannot find anything wrong with her. She was perfectly happy at school until three months ago. What should I do?

A I am sure you have talked to her, but try again, explaining that you understand that she is worried or scared about going to school, but if she tells you what is wrong, you could get it put right. Also, try to speak to her teacher, head teacher, school secretary and the dinner ladies. One of them might have a clue as to what has changed recently. Think too about what is going on at home. Is there any kind of upset in the family that could be the reason why she wants to stay at home with you all the time? If you can be firm about school, coupled with love and concern, I think you will find the answer soon.

Q My 14-year-old son finds it difficult to keep up at school and has great problems with project work. He can't seem to come up with any ideas, but we don't like to help because it seems like cheating.
A It is one thing doing the work for your son, but quite another giving him some ideas and encouragement. Set aside 15 minutes each evening when he is doing a project to discuss ideas, aims, and any problems that he may be having. Just being there for him will give him the encouragement he needs. If you are concerned about him keeping up at school, speak to his head of year.

3
Bullying

One of the biggest causes of depression in children and young people is bullying. No child deserves to be bullied, and it is up to adults – whether they be parents, teachers, family or friends – to make sure that they are not.

One of the major problems is that bullying can go undetected by parents for years because either the symptoms are not recognized, or the child refuses to admit that there is anything wrong. Children who are being bullied have a miserable existence, which clearly they don't deserve. They grow up in fear, with low self-esteem, the inability to concentrate on their schoolwork, and have difficulty in forming friendships.

Lucy's story

My daughter Lucy could write her own book on the subject as she was bullied for the whole of the time she was at secondary school. We never knew, because threats that she would be killed if she ever told us made her too scared to ask for help. Here in her own words is Lucy's story:

Many people say that your school years are the best years of your life and that you should make the most of them. With some people this may be true, but it certainly wasn't for me. My school years were the worst years of my life.

You see, I was bullied badly at secondary school by a group of girls. They would call me names like 'Loner', 'Wuss', 'Saddo' and even 'Thicko'. They hit me, pushed me, threw things over me, and even tripped me up. I can remember many occasions very clearly as though they happened yesterday, and I would like to tell you about a few of them.

I can remember walking into a classroom where I did Latin. I sat down and got out my books. One girl came up behind me and, before I could do anything, she threw a bag of flour over my head and called me 'Saddo' and 'Loner'. I grabbed my stuff and ran out of the room crying. My teacher came running after me. He made me go back and sit in the classroom; he wouldn't even let me go and clean the flour out of my hair and off my clothes. I had to sit there for the rest of the lesson with everyone looking at me and laughing.

On another occasion, I was walking home from school when a girl came up behind me and pushed me. I went flying down the hill and badly cut my knees – and she walked off laughing. There was a lot of blood and pain as I walked home and it was unbearable. I cried and cried.

One of the worst occasions when I was bullied, I will never forget as long as I live. I had just come out of the classroom after having had German. The girl who was the ringleader of the bullies came up to me and pushed me up against some lockers. She started hitting me and then grabbed me around the neck. I couldn't stop shaking and I started crying. She then threatened me, saying, 'If you tell anyone that I bully you then I will kill you next time.' The next thing I knew, she was swinging me round and round and she threw me against the stone stairs where I hit my head. I pushed and pulled as much as I could and eventually got free. I ran and ran and hid in the corner of the playground. Oh how I cried, I couldn't stop crying or shaking for hours. I wasn't able to tell anyone because I was so scared.

The girls who bullied me made me so scared and lonely. Every lunchtime I would be too frightened to go into the canteen to eat my lunch because they would call me names and take my food. Instead I would walk around the playground by myself, often crying, and I would hide in the corner to eat my lunch or I would wait until I got home to eat it.

The day I left school was the best day of my life. I went home and threw my school uniform and books away. I have tried not to look back and to get on with my life. I have been to college and come out with a distinction in Hotel and Catering, and am now in my second year at university doing a BSc honours degree in Hotel and Catering Management. I am very happy now, but I will never forget what those girls did to me.

I found out about the bullying when Lucy, then aged 15, accompanied me to the Philippines on a conference trip. We had spent the afternoon as guests of St Rita's College for Girls, where Lucy was treated with great kindness.

Later that evening she was very upset and told my husband and I that she wished she never had to go back to school. She explained that she had been bullied, and could not understand how the girls could have been so nice to her that day, when at home they had made her life hell.

Once we knew, we acted swiftly. We contacted the school and, when they were slow to act, we got in touch with the head of the education department, the board of governors, and took advice from the police.

After five years, the bullying finally stopped. The main culprit was suspended, but avoided being expelled because her mother was very ill with cancer and it would have been too much.

Today Lucy is happy, but the scars from those years will never really go away.

Signs that a child is being bullied

Before we go any further, it is important to look at some of the signs or behaviour that may indicate whether a child or teenager is being bullied. Here are a few:

- Making excuses to stay away from school, or hanging around so that they go in late to avoid bullies.
- Being scared to travel or walk to school.
- Asking you to give them lifts to school.
- Taking a longer or different route to school.
- Often feeling sick, or having headaches or tummy ache.
- Falling behind with their schoolwork.
- Becoming withdrawn and possibly developing a stammer.
- Crying more often over little things and crying themselves to sleep.
- Avoiding certain lessons or days, e.g. games, swimming.
- Having nightmares or sleepwalking.
- A loss of appetite.
- Having unexplained damage to books and clothes.
- Having unexplained cuts, bruises and scratches.
- Coming home from school starving because their dinner money has been taken.
- Their possessions going 'missing', or continually losing their pocket money.
- Asking for money to pay bullies.
- Losing interest in things they used to enjoy.
- Refusing to admit anything is wrong.
- Temper flare-ups, abusive language and hitting out at siblings.
- Attempting suicide.

If you become aware of any of these signs, it is a good idea to ask your child if they are being bullied or threatened by anyone. The chances are that they will deny it, but at least they will know that you realize that something is wrong and it will open up the door for them to talk to you about it at some point, even if it is not straight away. Tell them that if they are being bullied, you can do something about it because bullies are weak, insecure people who crack up when they are found out. Most bullies surround themselves with 'bullying helpers'. These are children who join in the bullying because they are scared that *they* will be bullied if they don't. When the bullies are found out, these frightened souls quickly dissociate themselves and the ringleader is left to face the music alone.

Bullying and depression are very closely linked and it is important to consider this when you are worried that your child is unhappy or low. If you think your child is being bullied, you need to act swiftly. Don't avoid facing up to the situation by coming up with well-worn clichés such as 'stick and stones may break your bones, but words will never hurt you'. This is rubbish. Bruises fade, but the mental scars from being bullied and victimized don't. Neither should bullying be put down as being teased. Bullying is vicious taunts, not just a bit of a laugh.

Telling children that they have to stand up for themselves, to hit back harder, or that it is character-building doesn't work either. They need your help because they cannot cope any more, and it is up to you to see that they get it.

Bullying is not just about being punched and kicked: name-calling, unkind rumours, being ridiculed, being excluded and threats are all part and parcel of it. In fact, it is the ridicule, being 'sent to Coventry' and threats that seem to be the most difficult type of bullying to cope with. If and when you find out that your child is being bullied, it is important to try to stay calm. Assess what is going on and work out exactly what you are going to say to the school so that you can do it in a calm but very firm way.

Helping your child if they are being bullied

Bullying is a kind of brainwashing that leaves the child with low self-esteem and a feeling they deserve to be treated this way. One of the most important things that parents can do is to rebuild this confidence with lots of praise and love. Here are 15 ways you can help your child if they are being bullied:

1 Approach the school and, if necessary, the school governors and

local education department (I cover this in more detail below).

2 Assure your child that you love them and that you are on their side.

3 Help them to understand that the bullying is not their fault.

4 Find time to talk to them. Discuss how they feel and share ideas for overcoming the bullies.

5 If it is possible, accompany them to and from school if this is what they want.

6 Explain that bullies get bored if they don't get the response that they expect (i.e. crying or fear). Suggest walking away if your child is upset.

7 Help your child to have pre-prepared responses to the most regular taunts. They don't have to be funny, but it helps to have something to say in reply and it makes the victim feel more in control.

8 Practise assertiveness techniques with your child. Get them to say NO very loudly and firmly and then walk away. It is hard to go on bullying if the victim doesn't get upset and simply walks off.

9 Praise your child whenever they achieve something. Letting them help with tasks around the home and giving them responsibility will boost their confidence.

10 Encourage your child to join clubs away from school where they can make new friends. Check to make sure that the bullies don't attend.

11 Victims of bullying often become withdrawn. Help your child to develop social skills by inviting other children to your home, but only one at a time in case there is any form of ganging up.

12 Take what your child tells you seriously and find out exactly what has been going on.

13 Don't promise to keep the bullying secret, but reassure them that you will get this problem sorted out once and for all.

14 If you feel that your child is depressed, take them to the doctor.

15 Finally, remember that this is *your* child and that you have every right to protect them from bullies. Don't be afraid to approach the school or do whatever it takes to get the bullying stopped.

Contacting the school and other official bodies concerning bullying

When you approach the school over bullying, be firm but keep calm. Don't get angry or aggressive or use insulting language, as it is important to keep a good working relationship with them. The moment that you learn that your child is being bullied, keep a diary with dates of all incidences and notes of any injuries – with photographs if possible. This will make it easier to check facts and to confront bullies. Also, keep a list of everyone you speak to about the bullying and copies of any letters you write or receive.

Once you are aware of bullying, contact the class or form teacher and request a meeting. Ask for an investigation and make a follow-up appointment for a week later to discuss the results and to find out whether the school has taken any action and if it has been successful. It might also be a good idea to discuss the situation with the year head if your child is at secondary school.

If the bullying continues, make an appointment to see the head teacher. Go armed with a list of questions you want answered and ask to see the school's 'discipline and anti-bullying policy'. A lot of parents find it advantageous to take a friend or relative to such a meeting for support, and as a witness to what has been said and what the meeting has achieved. The head teacher should agree to see you, but if not you will have to write to them.

The board of governors is the next step if the bullying continues. The name and address of the chairperson will be available from the school secretary. If a solution is still not forthcoming, then complain in writing to the director of education at your local council. You can get the name by telephoning the council and your letter should start 'I am writing to make a formal complaint'. Send it by recorded delivery and keep a copy. If you wish to complain to the Secretary of State for Education, your county councillor or Member of Parliament, you are able to do so. It may be possible to make an appointment to see your MP at his/her local surgery.

Try not to be put off if things don't seem to be getting sorted out as quickly as you hoped. Some acts of bullying can be singled out and dealt with almost immediately; others will take considerably longer. However, there are still schools that go on the defensive and are reluctant to admit that there is a bullying problem in the school. Teachers may also try to blame the victims for the bullying. This is very wrong, so don't be fobbed off with excuses or vague promises. It is not the victim's fault, and it is up to the school to sort the problem out. Make it very clear that you won't stand by and let your child be bullied, and you won't let the matter drop until it is resolved.

The school has a 'duty of care' towards its pupils, and bullying can affect a child's education. It also has a duty to provide adequate and efficient education, and you have the right to say if you feel that it is failing your child in this 'duty of care'. If you feel that this is the case, you can convey this in writing to the governing body of the school. It is legally bound to listen to your complaint and to treat it reasonably within the law.

In the United Kingdom, under section 36 of the Education Act of 1944, you are not bound to send your child to school, but parents do have a legal duty to see that their child receives adequate full-time education suitable to their age, ability and aptitude. This means that your child can be educated at home, or that you can remove your child from school until the bullying is stopped so long as you look after your child's educational needs. You could ask for home tuition from the local authority, but this will only be available if there are enough resources. Advice on home education can be sought through the Home Education Advisory Service by writing with a large stamped addressed envelope for a comprehensive information pack (PO Box 98, Welwyn Garden City, Herts AL8 6AN).

For advice on bullying, contact Kidscape, a non-profit-making registered charity that teaches children about personal safety, and addresses the problems of bullying for both parents and children. You can contact them in writing at 2 Grosvenor Gardens, London SW1W 0DH, or by telephoning between 10.00 a.m. and 4.00 p.m. Monday to Friday (020 7730 3300). If you prefer, you can e-mail them at info@kidscape.org.uk, or visit their website (www.kidscape.org.uk).

How children can help themselves if they are being bullied

We have covered how you as a parent can help your child to beat the bullies, and now we are going to look at ways in which children can help themselves.

First, make sure that they realize that they are *not* to blame for the bullying. Bullies enjoy the feeling of having power, but underneath there is usually a very unhappy person. Bullies are often being abused or ill-treated themselves, and have very little sense of self-worth. Others are spoilt at home and expect always to get their own way. The bully sees someone who is doing better than them or is different, and who they feel they can control, and this makes them feel good about themselves. The following points may help your child to overcome bullying:

- Stay in a group or a crowd whenever possible. Bullies usually pick on children who are on their own.

- Try to ignore or laugh at teasing or nasty comments. The bullies want you to be scared, and if they don't get the reaction that they want, they may soon get bored.
- Shout NO or GO AWAY as loudly and as angrily as you can. Bullies don't like aggression thrown in their direction, or attention drawn to them and what they are doing.
- Tell as many people (family, friends and teachers) what is going on. Ask for help.
- Arrange to travel to and from school with a friend.
- If you can, walk away quickly whenever bullying starts; if not, shout as loudly as you can to attract attention to what is going on.
- If you are threatened and being asked to give the bully money or possessions, do so. Your safety is more important than possessions.
- You don't deserve to be a victim of bullying, so be determined not to be one.
- Look for the good things in yourself.
- Try to make other friends, both within and outside school.

What schools can do about bullying

Finally, we will look at what schools themselves can do to counteract bullying:

- Have a clear-cut anti-bullying policy with guidelines and proce- dures for dealing with it.
- Encourage children and students to speak up if they witness bullying.
- Have a 'Bully Box' in school where pupils can put a note about what is happening.
- In class, encourage discussions – with role play – about bullying.
- Set up 'bullying counsellors' and forums where pupils can contribute ideas on how to counteract bullying and what punish- ment this should receive.
- Conduct surveys, particularly in the playground, to see if there is a problem.
- Have a list of school playground rules, with different parts of the playground used for ball games, and other parts designated quiet areas.
- Give each child a copy of the rules to sign so that they know what the rules are.
- Have adequate playground supervision.

- Deal with bullying as quickly as possible.
- Arrange for known bullies to leave school later than those who they have been bullying.
- Tell all pupils from day one that bullying will not be tolerated – that everyone has a responsibility to make sure that it does not happen in their school, and to speak up and stop the bullies.

Racial bullying

Racial bullying can be very difficult to deal with. Pupils need to learn that everyone is entitled to their own culture and religion and that discrimination is wrong. The Race Relations Act of 1976 states that schools and governing bodies have a duty to ensure that students do not face any form of racial discrimination, including attacks and harassment. Racial bullying includes any hostile or offensive action against people because of their skin colour, cultural or religious background or ethnic origin. It can include:

- Insulting or degrading comments, name calling, gestures, taunts, insults or jokes.
- Offensive graffiti.
- Humiliating, excluding, commenting, ridiculing or threatening.
- Making fun of the customs, music, accent or dress of anyone from a different culture.
- Refusal to work with or co-operate with others because they are from a different culture.

All teaching staff and governors need to be trained in issues relating to racial equality.

Bullying and depression can be so closely linked that it is sometimes one of the first things that should be considered if your child or teenager becomes withdrawn and unhappy. Solve the bullying and you are well on the way to getting rid of the depression.

Questions and answers

Q I think my daughter, Amber, is being bullied at school. The other day she went out with her friend and came back in tears. She would not tell me what was wrong, so in the end I gave up. Soon afterwards another girl from her class phoned up. I answered the phone and gave it to Amber. When she put the phone down, she was again upset. This time she told me what was wrong. The girl had asked Amber why she wasn't talking to the other girl and Amber said that she was. The girl who phoned up swore at Amber and slammed the phone down. Now she doesn't want to go to school any more and says she is being bullied. What should I do?

A Friends do fall out and this may be a one-off tiff that will sort itself out very quickly. If you feel that it is an ongoing thing, then go to the school and see Amber's head of year. Schools have bullying policies and a duty to make sure that any victims of bullying get the protection they need. Don't encourage Amber to stay at home after this one incident. Give her reassurance that she was right to tell you what was going on and that it is this other girl who is in the wrong, not her. Bullies crumble pretty quickly when they think that adults are on to them, so don't be afraid to speak to the school and don't be fobbed off.

Q I am a parent of two girls at our local school. I am also a parent governor. Recently I have witnessed two acts of bullying outside the school gates before and after school. I have also been told of other acts by parents. All of these cases of bullying have happened to, and been by, pupils of the school. I know who they are but I do not know the bullies' parents. Should I tell the teachers of the pupils involved?

A Having been a parent who was unaware that her child was being bullied for several years, I think you should speak up. My daughter put up with vicious bullying, too scared to say a word to her teachers or me until she was 15. I was horrified, not only to find out that bullying had gone on, but that she could have kept it to herself for so long. The reason she gave was that she was scared and did not want to worry us. You are in an enviable position as a parent governor, not only to speak of what you have seen, but also to do so on behalf of the other parents. Tell the school immediately, giving names. The school should then deal with this and contact both sets of parents. It might also help if you ask for the subject 'school bullying code of practice' to be put on the agenda of the next school governors' meeting. If you wanted to alert the parents of the children who you saw being bullied, probably the best way to deal with this would be to say 'I was really upset to see your daughter being bullied the other day. Is there anything I can do to help?' The parent is then likely to ask you who the perpetrators of the bullying were and the best reply you can give is, 'I think you should speak to your daughter and ask her or the school, who are aware of the incident.' Then let them deal with the school. An excellent source of help and information on bullying is Kidscape, and you can visit their website (www.kidscape.org.uk).

Q I have a beautiful seven-year-old daughter who has dyslexia. Bullying has been part of Lauren's school life since day one. Her speech has been slow to develop, although she has just about caught up now. During the past few weeks she has been taking money to school, telling me it is for drinks at lunchtime, but it came to my attention at the weekend that Lauren is being physically abused by four girls on a daily basis, and the money is being taken from her. I have been to the school on several other occasions about different incidents, but always seem to be fobbed off with promises that it will be looked into. Nothing is ever done! Can I withdraw Lauren from school until this matter is dealt with? Where do I stand? I cannot keep watching this happen.

A I was horrified to hear what has been happening to Lauren at school, especially as she is so young and therefore at a disadvantage to start with. The time has come for action. Go to the school straight away and ask to see the head teacher – don't be fobbed off, even if you have to wait. State clearly what has been happening and your disquiet of previous incidents not being resolved to your satisfaction. Say that if the matter is not dealt with at once, you will be writing to the school governors and the education department to make a complaint about their bullying policy and the way you feel they are letting your child down. Listen to what the school has to say as they may be dealing with the situation in their own way, which may seem rather slow to you. As for withdrawing your child from school, you have a legal right to do this. If this is just for a short time while the bullying is being sorted out, then see your doctor and ask if you can have a letter to give to the school that says something to the effect that your child is suffering from stress due to bullying. If you intend the absence from school to be more long term, then you need to make other provisions for her education, which could include a new school or home tuition.

I would like to finish this chapter with a second letter that I was happy to receive from Lauren's mum:

Dear Vicky
Thank you for your advice. I went to Lauren's school yesterday and spoke with the head. I explained everything that Lauren had endured and told her that she would not be returning to school until

the matter is dealt with. The headmistress called a meeting with six girls involved with the bullying, and even more children came up with more incidents that Lauren was put through on a daily basis. For example, she was made to walk the entire lunch hour, and if she did stop walking she would be pushed, her hair pulled, and smacked. The girls in question admitted that they had done this and much more.

We have had another meeting today and Lauren came with me. The children were brought into the office and apologized. The matter of the money being taken from her is still being dealt with, but I had the mother of one of the girls approach me this morning to apologize. I then received a letter from another one of the girls' mothers apologizing and inviting Lauren over for tea.

I will be collecting her every day for lunch for the next few weeks so that she can build up her confidence again and face them during lunchtime. I wouldn't say that the matter is completely laid to rest, but we have made a start and I want to thank you for your time – and to encourage other parents to make a fuss if their child is being bullied. Our children trust us and rely on us for their well-being and happiness. I just hope that Lauren has learnt that I will not let her down and I will always be there to help her.

4

Parental pressure

In this chapter we look at children whose parents put too much pressure on them to succeed, which leads to many of them suffering stress and depression.

In the course of my work as an agony aunt I receive countless letters and e-mails from parents of children as young as five or six who are so uptight about their child's progress at school that they are making themselves stressed as well as their children.

It is perfectly natural to want the best for your children and, yes, there are times when there is good cause to complain to the school if you feel your child's best interests are not being looked after. The trouble is there are far too many parents who are convinced that they either have a five-year-old genius on their hands, or who are determined that their child will outshine the rest of the class come hell or high water.

What they fail to understand is that children develop at their own pace, and a slow learner may streak ahead by the age of eight or nine, and a fast starter often levels out.

My daughter could read fluently by the age of four and a half, and her friend couldn't read at all. On Sundays my daughter would sing in church using the hymn book, and there would be her friend with the hymn book upside down pretending that she could read. Yet they left primary school at much the same standard, did equally well at secondary school, and both went to university and got good jobs. My daughter may have seemed much cleverer than her friend to begin with, but her friend developed in her own time and soon caught up.

There are far too many young children who are doing homework and being coached at home either by their parents or by a private tutor. Jessica, aged seven, was one of these:

Jessica's mother contacted me to say that she was concerned about her daughter because she had become withdrawn, tired and cried a lot. It seemed that they felt Jessica was a very gifted child, far more capable than the school gave her credit for, and that she was not being stretched enough. So on three evenings a week, Jessica went straight from school to private tuition, and on Saturday mornings she had coaching for maths. The aim was to get her a scholarship to a private school that would realize her potential. On top of this there were gymnastic lessons two nights a week, spellings after school to learn, and reading sessions with her mum before bed. Even the time journeying to school was used to test her on her spellings. No wonder Jessica was showing classic signs of being depressed.

There was never any let up, time to play, or be a child. Life for Jessica, and others like her, was a nightmare. She couldn't cope with the pressure that was coming at her from all sides.

I asked Jessica's mum if she worked, and she told me she was a cashier in a bank. I then went on to ask her how she would feel at the end of each day if she had to go on to another job, and then had to do more banking work in the evenings – because this in effect was what she was expecting Jessica to do. Reluctantly, she told me that this was what the school had said to her. Her teachers were concerned that Jessica wasn't mixing with the friends she used to mix with and was falling asleep in class.

Jessica's mum had always had good intentions, but had let things get out of hand in her quest for her daughter to achieve.

Simon's case was very similar, except that he constantly complained of stomach aches and feeling sick; he also cried a lot. He was seven, and liked school, but his mother would go every week to the school to check his progress and, despite being told by his teachers that he was one of the brightest in the class, she would put pressure on him to do even better. The poor little chap had his nose to the grindstone, from the moment he came home from school until bedtime, with test papers and extra tuition from his parents. Being ill meant they left him alone, but as the number of days he had off increased, the school suggested he should see the school doctor and maybe a school psychologist. His mother was horrified at this, but she did take him to see their GP, who diagnosed him as suffering from both stress and depression.

Giving children time to relax

We have to remember that children can't cope with all this pressure; it just isn't fair. They need time to enjoy their childhood and not to be pushed to the limits to satisfy their parents' ambitions for them.

What has happened to all the 'family times', when children came home to relax and enjoy themselves? For some children these have gone for ever, to be replaced by hard work and constant study.

However, going out for walks, to the library, swimming and doing things together after school are just as important. Our children are little for such a short time, and their childhood should be special, not snatched away from them.

When my children were little I always tried to make the time between the end of the school day and bedtime special – sometimes we would go to the park, other days we would make biscuits, create things out of clay, or just sit as a family and watch the television and talk until their dad came in, when we had our evening meal. There was Brownies, Cubs, netball and football, and in the summer we would drive to their dad's company to swim in their rather chilly pool, or to watch him play cricket or tennis. My husband and I worked in the garden while the children played, and at least twice a week we would let them go to bed later than usual so that we could drive to the Thames to watch the boats go through Shepperton Lock or to stroll around Hampton Court, which they really enjoyed. Socializing and being part of a family is an education in itself.

Children spend at least six hours a day at primary school and, in my opinion – based on my counselling experience – this is enough. They don't need to come home to more work. Yes, there are gifted children who do need a specialized education, but the majority will do just fine, with love, encouragement and no pressure!

There are times, though, when parents are right to worry, and extra help may be appropriate. For instance, not every child picks up reading as quickly as the others, and listening and reading together will give them the confidence that they might otherwise lack. Try reading alternate pages, and afterwards they might like to do a drawing to illustrate how they see the story. You can never read enough to your children, and the more they take a turn the better.

After-school guidelines at primary level

Of course, many parents have to work very long hours just to make ends meet, but for those who *are* at home and have the time, it is worth looking at how you use this after-school time. The following may be helpful as a guideline:

4 p.m.: Arrive home, give your children a drink and a snack, and use the next 15 to 20 minutes as listening time. Some children might not want to talk about their school day, but for others it is important. Try your best to give them your full attention, which you may not be able to give them at other times.

4.30 p.m.: Play or watch television, or go for a walk or visit the park.

5.30–6.00 p.m.: Teatime. Make sure that you sit together at the table, rather than watching television.

6.00–7.00 p.m.: Depending on age, bathtime followed by reading together, or you telling them a bedtime story.

7.30–8.00 p.m.: Unless you are doing something special, make sure they have a regular bedtime. This gives them boundaries, a sleep pattern, and gives you time to relax after they have gone to bed.

Pay no heed to the 'school gates gossip'!

Don't listen to the 'school gates gossip', where other mothers expound on how well their child is doing. It will only get you worrying if you feel your child is not doing as well. Remember what I mentioned before – children learn and develop in their own time. The school should tell you if there are any problems, but if you have any cause for concern, go in and see the teacher and get the reassurance that you need. This applies to all learning difficulties, and also if you suspect that your child might be dyslexic. Remember there is a vast difference between helping your child and putting so much pressure on them that they become depressed.

When children reach secondary school, parental pressure can really build up. Add to this the pressures they get from school, and this can often become a sure route to disaster and depression. This especially applies to homework and exams.

Parents and homework

There are a lot of parents who seem to take on the responsibility for the homework the child is set. Instead of leaving them to get on with it and giving them a bit of help when asked, they insist on planning the structure of each subject with their child, and overseeing it to the extent that it ends up virtually being their work that is handed in, not their child's. Instead of the half-hour that is allotted for each subject, these parents have their offspring working for hours on end in an attempt to make sure that they are seen by their teachers to be able to produce good work on their own. What they don't realize is that they are making things very difficult for their child at school because they cannot maintain the standard of their homework in their day-to-day classwork, and it also gives the teacher the wrong impression of the amount of work that can be done in the time set for each subject. The teachers have no way of knowing that they may be setting too much homework, or how much a child can cope with, unless parents tell the child to stop at the end of the set time, and then sign the 'homework diary' and explain this. I recently heard of a friend who told me that she was giving up her part-time job in the evening, even though her husband was at home, because she had to help her son with his homework. This is not what homework is meant to be about!

Tips for exams and revising

Exam time, particularly when it is GCSEs or A levels, bring its own pressures. There is a feeling that it is a 'now or never' situation, and that can affect both the student and the parents. The youngsters often find it difficult to apply themselves to revision; many keep putting it off until it is a last-minute shambles. Who can blame them – it is not easy to take exams in your stride or be super-efficiently organized. It is at this time that youngsters can benefit from advice and guidance from their parents, but not pressure.

Revising flat out won't do them any good, so encourage them to organize their time so that they do their revision but then take time out to see their friends and to socialize. Trying to cram everything into their heads from their notes or textbooks won't work. A note system on cards for each subject, or in a notebook with headings, would be much better. Under each heading they should have some concise notes that will remind them of this part of their work. These can be read through, and added to, and are far more likely to be remembered. Some students find recording notes on cassette is also a good way to learn, as they can listen to it any time they want to. Here are 20 tips that you can pass on to your teenagers that will hopefully help them to avoid exam stress:

1 It is important to plan your exam day so that you don't get flustered. The night before each exam, get everything you need ready, making sure you have enough pens, pencils and ink cartridges, and that the battery in your calculator isn't about to pack up. The same applies to your watch if it has a battery – you need to know exactly how much time you have left during the exams.

2 Make sure you get to bed early so that you get a good night's sleep. You don't want to be yawning all through the exams. Stop revising at least two hours before you go to bed, otherwise your mind will be buzzing all night and you won't sleep. Remember to set your alarm clock.

3 Get up early so that you have plenty of time to get ready. You don't want to have to run for the bus or worry about being on time for the exams. Have some breakfast even if you don't normally do this, and be sure you have something to drink. Your body needs plenty of fluids to be able to function properly.

4 Wear comfortable clothes and shoes to suit the temperature in the exam room. I know the majority of schools insist on school uniform being worn, but try to make your clothes as comfortable as you can within this. If you are allowed to go mufti, this isn't the day to be fashion-conscious. It's about comfort. Flat shoes not heels please, girls!

5 It is very important during the exam time to eat regularly and properly even when you don't feel like it. Snacking isn't a good idea. You need a balanced diet to get the best out of your brain cells. They need all the help they can get!

6 When you get to school, don't join in conversations with groups who are determined to make the most of the stress of the exams. You know the kind. They say things like, 'Did you know they put trick qustions in the exam papers?' or 'I know I am going to fail'. The truth is everything in the exam paper you will have covered at some point, and these silly people are just trying to get everyone else as wound up as themselves!

7 Feeling nervous and sick in the pit of your stomach? Unclench those hands, close your eyes, and take a few slow deep breaths. Tell yourself you deserve to do well and you *are* going to do well. This is just an exam that will be over in a very short time and it isn't worth making yourself feel ill. Believe me, it can work!

8 Spend time reading the exam paper right the way through before you start to answer any of the questions. Weigh up which ones you feel are your strongest areas, and start with these. Don't agonize over individual questions. Move on, and then go back to those you are not sure about and attempt them again.

9 When you come out of an exam, don't look up the answers to see if you got them right or worry about what you did. This exam is now in the past and it is time to concentrate on the next one.

10 Plan your revision in between your exams so that you avoid last-minute revision before going into an exam.

11 Try to relax in between exams. A lot of people find sport is a good way to switch off for a while. Or see your friends, go to the shops, listen to music – it doesn't matter what you do so long as you take time out for yourself. Don't sit cooped up in the house all the time. Get out and get some fresh air.

12 Don't succumb to outside pressure. You may have been promised a new computer or a bike by your parents or grandparents if you do well, but at the end of the day these are your exams, your results, your future, and you can only do your best.

13 If you have a Saturday or evening job, think about whether this is going to put too much pressure on you during exam times. You may need to juggle your hours around to fit in with your revision and exams or take the occasional day off. This isn't being lazy – it is about getting the balance right.

14 Remember it is never too late to get advice. If you are worried about your revision, or a particular subject, phone the school. If you are only going in at exam times, ask if you can come in and see your tutor. They will be in school teaching the other years anyway.

15 Find a peaceful spot to do your revision. If you can't do this at home, go to the library or perhaps to your grandparents' home if they live nearby. If the weather is good, try revising outside. (I did most of mine sunbathing in the park!)

16 Talk to your best friends. It is good to share the laughs and the worries, and it gets things into perspective.

17 Keep thinking about those long lazy summer holidays ahead – that will get you through!

18 It is never a bad thing to have contingency plans, especially when you are doing A levels. I am sure you will do well in your exams, but life doesn't end with these exams. There are always re-sits, a job, or you can take a year out to travel or do voluntary work.

19 Plan a reward for yourself so that you have something to look forward to at the end of the exams. This can be anything from a day out with friends, to seeing a film that you have been wanting to see for a long time or, if you are really lucky, a holiday.

20 Finally, try to stay positive. Yes, negative thoughts might creep in, but remember everyone else is just as worried as you are. If possible, trust your parents and talk things through with them. Winston Churchill passed no exams at all, and he became one of the greatest Prime Ministers of all time – *so stop worrying*!

Parental pressure and exams

Many parents offer treats and rewards as encouragement to get their children to revise and do well in exams. This is fine so long as there isn't a nasty sting in the tail, with recrimination and the piling on of guilt if they don't achieve what you expect.

PARENTAL PRESSURE

The sad fact is that thousands of teenagers get so stressed at exam times that many of them go on to suffer with depression. This is certainly not what exams are intended to invoke, or what parents want for their offspring. It is a time when youngsters need protection as much as anything else; and a good balance between encouragement and knowing that they can only do their best will keep them from succumbing to too much stress.

If you as a parent have ever wished that you had gone to university but didn't have the chance, it is only natural to hope that your child will have that opportunity. However, problems arise when parents try to re-live their lives through their children, and push them into going to university when they don't want to go – for whatever reason.

The other side of the coin of parents putting pressure on their children to succeed are those who indirectly put pressure on their children because they are not interested at all. They are too wrapped up in their own lives, leaving their children feeling they have dud parents who don't care and are not interested in them.

Kelly wrote to me in a dreadful state just before she started her GCSE exams. She told me she lived in a flat with her parents and younger sister and brother. Her parents never bothered to go to parents' evenings at school, and they showed no interest when she chose her options, or in the exams she was about to take. Revision at home was impossible as she shared a bedroom with her sister, who played in there most of the time. In the lounge the television was on day and night, and when she asked her mum if she could turn it off while she revised she was told not to be so selfish. Her parents liked to go to the pub and Kelly was expected to babysit regularly. Sadly, this didn't give her the time to revise either, as her brother had a behaviour problem and would play her up all the time their parents were out.

Kelly's best friend said she would ask her parents if she could come and revise at their house, but Kelly felt awkward about this. Seeing her friend's parents being helpful only made the situation at home worse, and she was embarrassed for them to know the reasons why she couldn't revise at home.

This is a different kind of pressure to that of parents over-eager for their children to do well, but it was one that caused Kelly to be depressed and harm herself. Even then, her parents didn't see what was going on and they got angry with Kelly – saying she always caused them grief and worry. Needless to say, Kelly didn't do well at

41

her exams, but she did get into college and do an NVQ in catering. I hope that she will be able to build on this for the future.

Parents who pressurize teenagers into particular careers

Finally, we look at parents who pressurize their teenagers into careers that they don't want. Often it is a case of parents wanting them to go into the family business or what they consider to be 'safe jobs'. They mean well, but they forget that they are not the ones having to get up each day and do a job that they didn't choose, and possibly hate.

I receive lots of letters from teenagers who know what they want to do, but are being pushed by their parents in another direction:

Lisa wanted to go to stage school, but her parents thought it would be a very insecure career choice as so many actors are out of work. Instead her mum arranged for her to go for an interview for a job at the insurance company where she worked. Although Lisa didn't want to work there, she accepted the job when it was offered to her because she didn't want to upset her mum.

Six months later, she was so depressed that she was put on antidepressants and her doctor arranged for her to have counselling. It was through this that Lisa decided she had to take control of her own destiny. She told her mum she was applying for the next entry to stage school, and then she worked as a waitress until she was accepted. She started later that autumn and has been there for nearly a year now. Her parents are still worried about the insecurity of her wanting to be an actress, but are relieved that Lisa is no longer depressed.

In most cases, this sort of pressure is unintended and not recognized by the parents themselves. They simply want the best for their children and don't realize the strain they are putting them under. It is up to all of us as parents to find the right balance between guidance and taking too much control. Unless we can do this, we run the risk of destroying our children's lives when in fact we only want them to be happy.

Questions and answers

Here are two questions from my mailbag that illustrate how teenagers feel about parental pressure:

Q   Can you help me? I want to go to college to do hairdressing, but my dad says 'no way'. He thinks hairdressing is for girls, not boys, and he is trying to get me to take up car mechanics so that I can work in his garage. I don't want to. Mum says she is keeping out of the argument.

A   A lot of the world's best hairdressers are men, so I think your dad is a bit off-beam here. I also wonder who cuts his hair. Is it a man? Hairdressing has become very much a unisex thing over the past few years, with men and women training to cut hair of both sexes and salons opening to cater for everyone. I think your dad is a bit disappointed that you don't want to follow him into the motor trade, but at the end of the day you are the one who has to do the job and it has to be something you will enjoy. Talk to your year head or careers adviser, and enlist their help in getting the message over to your dad that this is what you intend to do. You may have to stand your ground, but don't be pushed on to a course that you know will be wrong for you. Don't argue, just be firm.

Q   Why can't parents leave teenagers to choose for themselves what they want to do? I haven't even finished my GCSEs – which I am struggling with – and they are putting pressure on me to stay on to take A levels and go to university. I lie in bed worried sick about failing because of upsetting my parents. My dad said he never got the chance to go to university, and that I must go. I don't say anything because they are so wrapped up in what they want that they wouldn't listen.

A   This kind of pressure is hard on teenagers, and every year I get dozens of letters from students of all ages who are stressed, saying much the same as you are. It isn't right for parents to try and live their youth again, or their dreams, through their children, but I am sure this is about your parents wanting what they see as the best for you, and you cannot blame them for this. You say you haven't talked to them about this, so how can they begin to understand how you feel? Don't judge them without giving them the chance to listen. Maybe they are trying to give you dreams to hang on to as well, but begin by talking to them.

5

Children and teenagers need to feel good about themselves

Self-image is very important to young people, with many hating their bodies, especially as they reach puberty. Hating themselves will make them depressed. Many are scared of the changes that puberty brings because they don't understand what is going on. In this chapter we will look at recognizing when your child needs advice on issues related to growing up.

Explaining the facts of life to children

This principle particularly applies to explaining the facts of life rather than letting them get information from elsewhere that they don't understand. Some parents ignore the subject completely through sheer embarrassment; others want to get it done and dusted as quickly as possible and don't give any thought as to whether the time is right for their child.

Answering questions as and when they come up is the best way to go about things. It gives the child a sense of security and enables them to discuss any worries they have rather than becoming depressed. Try to give honest answers, and only to those questions they ask. Don't go any further because they may not be ready to do this. You may also find that they ask the same questions a few days, or weeks, later. This is quite common as they may not have understood the first time. If you find it difficult and get tongue-tied, don't worry, you are not alone. Children need to be told the facts of life in simple terms. Start by explaining that a baby needs a mother and a father because it is made from part of each of them. The mother has the egg, but it can't grow until the part from the father, which is called a sperm, reaches it. Once it does, the two join together and a baby grows.

Explain that to make a baby a couple have to be very close and to kiss and cuddle a lot. When they do this, say that the father's penis (you can use whatever word your child is familiar with for this) gets stiff and erect because this is the way he puts the sperm into the mother, who has a special baby passage called a vagina. Make sure that you explain to your child about the nice feelings that go along with this, and that Mum and Dad enjoy it (because it can sound a bit

44

frightening to some children). Tell them how the sperm reaches the egg and makes it grow, and that for nine months the baby grows inside the mother and is then born through the special baby passage.

This is a very simple explanation and you can enlarge on it in any way that you feel comfortable with. It can also be the basis of explaining contraception at a later date. Explain that adults make love regularly, not just when they want a baby, and that preventative steps have to be taken otherwise women would be getting pregnant all the time. You can also label the parts of the body in any way you want, so long as your child understands you. Many parents prefer to use nicknames for sexual parts, but remember there is nothing dirty or rude about using the correct terms. You will find your children probably ask questions at the most difficult times for you to answer. I know one of my boys did when he was about four. We were walking around the supermarket when he suddenly said very loudly, 'How do babies get into your tummy?' Other shoppers looked on with amused smiles as if to say, 'Get out of that one if you can!' I said to my son, 'That is a very good question, but I think we should talk about it when we get home.' On arriving home I broached the subject and gave him a simple answer: that babies grow from an egg in a mummy's tummy. To which he replied, 'What time does children's television start?' (About a year later he asked again, and seemed more interested at that point.)

Discussing menstruation

Even if you find it difficult, it is really important that you explain to girls in good time about periods – although not too early. A child under seven may say they understand, but any kind of bleeding is scary, and they may be frightened at the thought of this happening to them. At seven or eight a child might see her mother's pads or tampons, perhaps when they are bought at the supermarket, and may ask what they are. You don't have to answer there and then. Say you will talk about it when you get home, and don't forget to do this. The same applies to boys – they should know about periods as well.

To explain about periods, start by saying that all girls have special egg-making organs called ovaries, just as all boys have sperm-making organs called testicles, and that sometime between the ages of 9 and 16 (sometimes a bit later) the egg-making organs in a girl start to work and each month an egg is released that could become a baby. This travels along a tube to an organ called the uterus (womb), where a nice thick lining has been growing during the month for the egg to become embedded if it has been fertilized by the man's sperm. If the egg is not fertilized, then the body gets rid of the egg (which, incidentally, is so small that you can't see it without a microscope) along with the lining of the uterus, so that the body can make a fresh one for the following month. This loss of blood is called a period.

You can explain that along with periods can come some discomfort and mood swings, but it is best to discuss these once your daughter has started her periods rather than worry her beforehand. Before the periods start there are usually some signs over the previous months that signal that it will happen soon. Your daughter will notice changes in her body. She will get rounder hips, a more shapely waist, and her breasts will start to develop. Hair will start to grow under her armpits and she will also get pubic hair. For several months before her periods start, you can tell her that she may also notice a whitish discharge from her vagina and that some girls do get pre-period tummy aches as well.

Boys and puberty

Let us look at what happens to boys at puberty (the age varies from around 11 to 14 or even older). Usually it begins with a sudden growth spurt, and some boys can grow as much as 6 inches. Another area of growth is in the larynx, which grows and may become prominent. The effect of this is a change in the pitch of voice, and for a time the voice goes from high to low pitch until it settles down. When this happens, do remember not to tease!

Around about the same time the skin starts to change and becomes more coarse and hairier. This is particularly around the arms, stomach and sex organs. Other changes that the boy will notice is that the sex organs begin to grow. The scrotum and its enclosed testicles become heavier and larger, the penis thickens and becomes longer, and the skin around may darken in colour.

'Wet dreams'

When a boy reaches a certain weight, the endocrine system is triggered, the glands start to work and the testicles do their job, which is to produce sperm and the special liquid they live in called semen. Together this is stored in a special sac just behind the penis until it is thrown out of the body. This is where 'wet dreams' come into being. Once the testicles start working, they do so continuously. They don't store enough to fill the sac and then stop – they keep going! This means that every so often (maybe two or three times a week) it is released while the boy is asleep. Quite often this is accompanied by an exciting or sexual dream. If a young boy doesn't know about wet dreams and wakes to find his pyjamas wet, he may be worried. Some lads think they have wet themselves; others worry that they have something wrong with them. One lad wrote to me thinking he had cancer.

Wet dreams are one of the most difficult things parents find to talk to their children about. Many never get round to it at all, and this can lead to worry and anxiety for their sons who don't understand what is happening. Added to this, when they start to masturbate – as most young boys and girls do – they will often feel guilty. This can lead to problems throughout their lives that could have been avoided if only their mum or dad had been able to explain the normal functions and workings of their body.

Masturbation

Soon after wet dreams begin, boys find that masturbating is pleasurable. Virtually all boys and girls masturbate and there is no shame in this, even though many parents prefer not to think about it in relation to their own children.

Although it is usually accepted that young boys masturbate, this is not always the case for girls. Very few girls will actually admit to masturbating, but the truth is that almost all girls do and there is nothing wrong with this. Masturbation in boys and girls is natural and normal.

Once in a sexual relationship, the need to do this diminishes, but a lot of people both young and old continue to masturbate whether they are in a relationship or not. Older men and women worry a lot about masturbating, thinking it is something that only young people do, but this isn't true. By discussing masturbation with your child you will be releasing them from any guilt about this in the future. Mutual masturbation is also a very normal part of a loving relationship. Contrary to old wives' tales, masturbation will not make hairs grow on the palms of your hands, or make you go blind or mad. Neither will it stop you being able to have a proper sexual relationship.

The good thing about masturbation, apart from the sexual release, is that it enables young people to get to know their bodies without embarrassment and to be aware of what is right for them sexually. It is not unhealthy or harmful. The downside is that youngsters can become withdrawn and depressed if they think what they are doing is dirty, perverted or wrong:

> Paul was a 12-year-old who wrote to me because he felt guilty about masturbating. So much so that he didn't mix with the others at school after hearing them say that masturbators were perverts. All the others were probably masturbating too, yet none of them felt able to admit it. By sticking a 'perverted' label on masturbation, they were giving out the message that it was something they wouldn't do. Paul became very withdrawn and depressed and wrote to me asking if he could be cured of this habit. It hadn't helped when his mother had told him that he was dirty when she caught him touching himself, because it felt nice, when he was about seven. He could still feel the sting of guilt that had hit him then.
>
> I wrote back to Paul explaining about wet dreams and masturbation, which he said made him feel better about himself. He told me that he still joined in when the others called masturbators 'perverts', because he didn't know what else to do, but at least he knew he was normal and not 'dirty'.

Depression and puberty

Around about the time of puberty, lots of youngsters get depressed – partly because they don't understand what is going on in their bodies, but also because the thought of making the transition from child to adult is frightening. Some children don't want to discuss sexual matters with their parents, and if this is the case you cannot force them to do so. However, if you are always there to listen and answer their questions throughout their lives, there is more chance that they will do so.

If your child has reached an age where you think they probably know all about sex anyway, you may feel it is too late to discuss it, but it isn't. They may have picked up a lot of information along the way, but there is nothing to say that they have the facts right. You could say, 'I know I should have spoken to you about sex before this, but I wondered if there was anything that you needed to talk to me about?' The chances are they will be so embarrassed that they will insist there isn't, but it will leave the door open in case they change their minds. If you are worried that your teenager may be, or is about to be, sexually active, then a direct question such as 'Do you know about contraception and safe sex?' is a good way to start. *You* may even learn something you didn't know from them!

Apathy and boredom in young people

Recognizing apathy and boredom in your children is difficult, but it is essential, as both can cause depressed feelings. Some children need more stimulation than others. Many make their own entertainment and social life with their friends, but there are some who are unable to do this. The dictionary definition of apathy is 'lack of interest', and this can be one of two things. It can either be not enough in their lives to keep them interested, or the loss of interest in things that they would normally enjoy. In the latter case, it would be described as becoming apathetic. Depression and apathy go hand in hand, so if you find your child has become apathetic this is something that you must consider.

There can be few parents who haven't heard the cry 'I'm bored', and every child gets bored at times. It is when it is continuous, though, that you have to keep a watchful eye. Boredom is associated with the feeling that everything is dull, tedious, monotonous and uninteresting; and negative thoughts are very closely associated with the signs of depression. Don't overlook these if your child is constantly withdrawn, moody and shows signs of being unhappy. Speak to your GP and get help. At the same time, try to stimulate interest by finding things that your child might enjoy. Doing things as a family is particularly helpful as it gives a feeling of belonging, and so is finding some of your time to spend just with them, without the rest of the family. Everyone needs to feel they are special, and parents who find time individually for their children will reap the benefits. As the parent of four children, I do know how difficult this can be. It is so easy to lump the family together and not recognize the individual needs of each child. Some definitely need more of your time than others.

Self-image and teenagers

Self-image and self-worth become increasingly important as teenage years progress – so much so that the slightest dent to the ego can cause emotions to run riot. Teenagers need to learn that they don't need other people's approval to be of worth, and it is harder for them than it is for the rest of us. What their friends think of their partners, clothes, family and lifestyle is all-important. In fact, it is what makes their life tick.

Any parent who has said 'it doesn't matter what your friends think' will quickly have been told that it does! However much you try to convince them otherwise, this statement will have no effect until your teenager is mature enough to realize it for himself or herself. In the meantime, all you can do is reassure them of your love, that the family needs them, and listen to them when they feel down. Sometimes that is all that is needed: they simply need to get their aggrieved feelings off their chest so that they can work things out in their own minds. You cannot do it for them.

Knowing you are there for them will make all the difference, even though they may not say anything. The vital thing to remember is to listen, and to try not to go on at them.

Teenagers and mood swings

We all get mood swings, but teenagers get them more than others; and although you may sympathize with them, it doesn't mean that you have to put up with rudeness or aggression to any other member of the family. When things are not going their way, teenagers tend to take their moods out on the family, and particularly the most vulnerable member. This may be their mum, who they think will put up with most things, or younger members of the family who cannot stand up for themselves.

A friend of mine told me that her youngest son's life had been made a misery when his 15-year-old brother's girlfriend went off with his best mate. Unable to do anything about this, and with his self-esteem in shreds, the older brother would take out his anger on Tim, who was only eight. My friend noticed bruises on his body and asked Tim how he had got them. Scared that he would get another thump from his older brother if he said anything, he lied and said he had fallen over in PE. Fortunately, his mother didn't believe him because there were too many bruises, so she confronted her older son who said 'Tim irritated him and got in his way'. Knowing the real reason, she ignored this, and told him that he wasn't in future to take out his anger on Tim about what had happened.

Eating disorders

Anorexia and bulimia

Because outward image is so important to youngsters, this is why so many girls worry about their bodies, with some becoming anorexic because they think they are fat. I have had a 16-year-old girl who was size 6, and weighed under 7 stone, sit in front of me and insist that she was fat and had to lose more weight. The fact that she was slowly killing herself was something that she wouldn't accept. She became bulimic and would binge on food, then made herself sick or took laxatives to get rid of the food. She ended up in hospital. Bingeing is often a way of coping with depressed feelings, but vomiting and purging leave feelings of guilt and wretchedness.

Most of us eat both because we have to and because we enjoy it. There are those, however, who go to extremes by eating too much or too little. Anorexics have a fear of fatness, so they starve themselves, lose excessive weight, and often exercise vigorously; consequently, their monthly periods may stop. It is estimated that anorexia affects 1 15-year-old girl in every 150. Nearly always it begins with the everyday dieting that is so much a part of many teenage lives. About a third of sufferers of anorexia have been overweight before starting to diet. Unlike normal dieting, which stops when the desired weight is reached, in anorexia the dieting and loss of weight continues until the sufferer is well below the normal limit for height and age. Many take slimming pills to keep their weight low and, although they may eat lots of fruit, vegetables and salad, they take in only a tiny number of calories.

As time goes on, the teenage anorexic girl may also make herself sick and use laxatives as a way of controlling her weight. This chaotic way of eating and controlling weight dominates many lives. Many sufferers of anorexia and bulimia have depressive feelings, especially in our western culture where being slim is equated with beauty. The first step in treating such disorders is to recognize the problem. The second is speed in getting help. The longer it goes unrecognized or ignored, the harder it will be to help.

Overeating

The other side of the coin is overeating and putting on a lot of weight; this can make the child unhappy and the victim of spiteful comments. Overeating applies equally to boys and girls and is often encouraged by parents who themselves are overweight and who encourage their children to eat too much – and the wrong things. I have lost count of the number of letters I have received from youngsters who are very overweight and dread going to school, and who have become depressed. It is a vicious circle. They comfort-eat because they are unhappy, which in turn makes them put on more weight and makes them even more miserable.

If you think your child has any sort of eating problem, don't ignore it.

Even if you are overweight, this doesn't mean that your child should be. See your GP and get help. If you are connected to the internet, you might also like to log on to the Eating Disorders Association (website at www.edauk.com) for more information. They also have a helpline on 01603 621 414 (open 9 a.m. to 6.30 p.m. weekdays), and a youth line for the under-18s, with trained youth workers to take calls, on 01603 765 050 (open 4 p.m. to 6 p.m. weekdays).

We all need to feel good about ourselves, and the same is true for our children. With our help, they can achieve this.

Questions and answers

Here are some relevant problems that I have received in my mailbag:

Q My four-year-old son saw me in the nude the other day, pointed at my breasts, and asked what they were. I was so embarrassed and told him to go back to bed, but now I feel guilty that I fobbed him off.
A Yours was a natural reaction when caught unawares. Don't worry about it, but be prepared for future questions and try to answer them as honestly as possible. In this instance, all you needed to say was 'they are breasts'. If he went on to ask 'what are they for?' your answer could be 'all ladies have them and use them to feed milk to their babies'.

Q I am 13 and very fat and ugly. I am 5 feet tall and weigh over 12 stone. I want to lose weight, but all our family are big eaters. Mum serves up huge meals and gets cross if anything is left. I told her that I want to lose weight, but she says she is not having me dieting at my age. Mum, Dad and my older brother weigh massive amounts more than me. Dad has a job getting clothes to fit him. At school I get called 'blob'. When we are in the showers I can hear the other boys laughing about me. I feel like killing myself. I am so depressed.
A You are right to be concerned about your weight, and just because the rest of your family are overweight doesn't mean you have to be too. If your mum won't listen, speak to your year tutor and ask if you can see the school doctor or nurse. Perhaps if someone else told your mum that you should lose weight, she might take notice. Talk to your mum again as well, and explain how unhappy you are. Smaller portions at each meal may be all that is needed to combat your weight, which isn't a lot to ask of your mum – and it may just encourage the rest of the family to do the same.

Q In a few days' time I will be 14. When PE comes I dread getting changed because I still don't wear a bra. All my friends wear them. All the boys know I am flat chested and they taunt me about it. I try to join in the joke, but it really hurts. I have lost all confidence in myself and I don't like wearing showy tops because I am afraid of what everyone thinks. Please, is there anything I can do to boost my confidence?

A I know how you feel because I was a late developer like you, and thought I would never get a bust. Don't get despondent, because things will change. You are not abnormal and gradually you will develop a bust. Don't take any notice of the boys; they are immature and their opinions count for nothing. Have a look around the shops at the padded bras. They come in really small sizes now in lots of pretty colours and I am sure you could get one that fits without looking fake. That would give you enough shape not to feel awkward. Lots of girls wear these and they look very attractive.

6

Dangerous situations and scared feelings in families

Geraldine heard her husband coming up the front path. It was 2 a.m. and she knew that he was drunk. Quickly she got her two young children out of bed and into the cupboard under the stairs where she thought that their father would not be able to get at them. She went to follow and hide with them, but she was not quick enough. The front door burst open. Within seconds, he was upon her, beating her unmercifully. The children, although scared, had crawled out of the cupboard and watched in horror as their mum crumpled to the floor bruised and bleeding.

This is a terrible story, but sadly one that too many children have to live with every day of their lives:

Michael, aged nine, was one such lad, whose father was constantly knocking his mother around. Because of this Michael suffered not only with asthma, but also with depression. It was difficult for his mother to get him to go to school most days and, when he did go, he would sit in the class in a world of his own, not participating or paying any attention to what was going on around him.

The school knew what went on at home because Michael had drawn pictures of his mum being hit by his dad. They had also seen injuries inflicted upon her and knew that on several occasions she had been in hospital. Despite all this, she refused to press charges against her husband and told people that he didn't mean to get angry with her. What she did not see, or closed her eyes to, was the effect that all this was having on Michael. Instead, she grew angry with him because she said he was difficult and badly behaved.

One day, after witnessing a particularly violent scene between his parents, Michael had a really bad asthma attack and collapsed. He was taken to hospital, along with his mother who had a broken jaw and a fractured skull. Even though he recovered from the asthma attack, it soon became apparent to the medical staff that Michael was very depressed and withdrawn. Social Services were called in, and it was decided that it was in Michael's best interest to be taken into care, with plenty of access for his mother. Over the next few months, Michael lived with foster parents, saw his mum regularly, and also visited a child psychologist. Slowly he became less withdrawn, more attentive in school, and his depression lifted. When I last heard from Michael's mum she told me that Michael was much happier, but wanted her to leave his dad – who was still beating her up – so that they could live together without him. Sadly, she hasn't had the courage to do this, and Michael is still with his foster parents.

Michael's mother and father would probably be the last people to admit that there was a dangerous situation in their family. To them, it is all part and parcel of everyday living and they closed their eyes to the effect that their violence was having on Michael.

Abuse and depression

This sort of thing happens behind closed doors in many families throughout the country. Whether the parents are drug addicts, gamblers, alcoholics or abusers, it does not matter, all of these affect the children and cause mental torment and depression. The trouble is that the parents are so wrapped up in themselves that they do not realize (or, in many cases, care) what they are doing to their children.

When I work on radio or television, it is not unusual to take calls during the programmes. Sometimes there is not enough time to take all the calls, or to get to grips properly with the problem that the person rang in with. When you speak to someone on air, it is extremely important that you remember that it may not be until they put the phone down that they realize they have revealed things about themselves to thousands, even millions, of people who are listening in. This can come as a terrible shock, especially if they are in the house alone, and have no one to reassure them. If I am worried, I always make a point of telephoning the person back after the programme to make sure that they are all right. It is called 'grounding' and it is very important, both in counselling and the work of an agony aunt. That is also why you have to be very careful what you put in reply to readers' letters, because you only know their side of the story and you must not be judgmental. They need reassuring advice.

It was after one such programme that I phoned Stephanie, an 18-year-old student. She was very agitated when she rang in, and although she told me that she was depressed, she also told me how wonderful her family life was. I talked to her on air about her depression, but her story just didn't add up. When I was off air, I felt very worried about her and called her back. When she answered the phone it was very strange, as if she had been expecting me to call her. The relief in her voice was very apparent, and gradually she told me what was causing her to be depressed:

From the age of nine, her father had been sexually abusing her. When she was 16, he went to work in Saudi Arabia, and for two years she was free from his perverted attentions. Twice over the years she had tried to tell her mum what was going on, but her mother called her a 'nasty liar'. Three weeks before she made the call to me, her father returned from abroad, apparently for good. Over the previous two years, she had always gone to stay with friends or her Nan when he had come back for a couple of weeks' holiday. Now she was in the house all the time, and so was he. The day before she spoke to me, her father had tried to rape her. When she resisted, he hit her, leaned over to the window sill where there was a potted plant, grabbed some of the soil from it, and forced it up into her vagina. She was beside herself with pain and fear, and then he raped her. The pain, she told me, was dreadful, and the soil caused her to bleed. 'It is still inside me,' she sobbed. 'Have you told your mother?' I asked. 'I have tried,' she said, 'but she did not want to hear a word against him.' I advised her to go to the police straight away, pack her things, and go to her Nan's or a friend. She said she would. She had a younger sister whom she was scared that he might be abusing as well.

I did not hear from Stephanie for over a year, and then I only got a short message from her that she had left for me at the radio station. The note read:

Dear Vicky,
It is me, Stephanie! Hi! Sorry that I have not been in touch, you have helped me a lot. Dad has gone to prison for what he did to my sister and me. Yes! He had got to her as well. My sister is still with Mum, but I live with Nan. I think that Mum hates me for what I have done, but I know that it was the right thing, even though he is my dad. I am going to college now. I still get times when I feel very depressed, but hopefully this will go away. Thanks,
Stephanie

Not long after this, I received the following anonymous poem from another young reader. The poem is called 'Abuse':

Abuse

When I was young my father abused me,
He used my love as a child
To suit his sick needs.
With a power driven sick man's greed.

He used my mother's love
To silence my cries,
He kept me tangled in his web of lies

I suffered pain and guilt and I carried the blame.
I lived in hell like a bottomless well
Going further down
I never thought I would surface,
Get out and feel solid ground.

My mother's love kept me alive inside.
She was there to ease the pain of everyday strains.

He was wrong to abuse me
And take my innocence and use me.
He took away my childhood
And replaced it with feelings that I should not have felt.
Anger, hurt, pain,
And never being allowed to be a child.

Paedophiles

However, it is not only parents who sexually abuse children. It is estimated that around 65 per cent of paedophiles (people who sexually abuse children) are known to the child – which is a very frightening situation.

Unlike the picture of paedophiles that many of us have, they come from all walks of life, professions, races and religious backgrounds. Although the majority of known paedophiles are male, there are women who abuse children as well.

One of the major problems is that paedophiles are good at making friends with children. They gain the child's trust by taking them out for the day, give them treats and gifts, or play sport and games with them. They can be family members, babysitters or close friends. Single-parent families are often targeted by paedophiles because they know that the mother may be having difficulty coping with the children on her own.

Most of us will have left our children with babysitters at some point. It is imperative that you know and trust the person you leave your children with, as according to Kidscape (the national charity for keeping children safe) 48 per cent of paedophiles found their victims through babysitting. Some 30 per cent of paedophiles had committed offences against 10 to 450 victims, and 70 per cent between 1 and 10 victims.

Be aware of those around your children – especially those who seem more interested in the children than in you, or who try to find ways of being with your children on their own.

Paedophiles find their victims by hanging around places where children enjoy going, or where they are likely to be, such as:

- Playgrounds
- Amusement arcades
- Swimming pools
- Parks
- Schools
- Fast-food restaurants
- Shopping centres
- Sports centres
- Waste grounds
- Lonely or isolated areas
- Burger bars
- Public toilets

You can help to keep your children safe by checking anyone who is left in charge of them or who wants to spend time alone with them, especially babysitters. Talk to other people who have employed them or who have let them look after their children.

Keeping your children safe

Discuss personal safety with your children, with particular emphasis on what to do if they feel unsafe or are approached by someone that they do not know or feel uneasy with. Tell them that if they find themselves in this kind of situation they should shout loudly and run away. Paedophiles do not like attention drawn to them. They should also tell you, or another adult whom they trust, as quickly as possible about their fears.

Children are often cajoled into keeping a secret by paedophiles, so make sure that your child knows the difference between 'safe' and 'unsafe' secrets. Tell them that a secret about a present or a party or a treat is fine, but that no one should ever ask them to keep kisses, hugs or touching secret. This also includes those that they know. They should tell you at once if this happens. If your children are old enough to be out and about on their own, buy them a travel card, and a phone card or a mobile phone, so that they can always keep in touch or get home.

With younger children, have a password, so that if anyone else collects them from school the person must always give the password so that the child knows that it is safe to go with them. If the person doesn't give the password, then tell your child that they should never go with them – but instead should go back into school and tell their teacher.

It is easy to get separated from your children in public places, so always arrange a meeting place in case you get parted. Tell your children never to get into someone's car unless this has been agreed with you, and if a person they don't know speaks to them, to pretend that they haven't heard and walk away as quickly as possible. Make it clear that they must never take gifts or sweets from strangers, and to be wary of public toilets – they should always go in with a friend.

We all make rules for our children's safety, but even the best-behaved children sometimes break them. Reassure your child that even if this happens, and they have found themselves in dangerous situations, they should *always* tell you and that you will never be cross.

Children and teenagers should always shout 'no' loudly and get away as fast as they can if someone tries to touch them. They need to run towards shops, or places with people. If they think that they are being followed, they should go into a shop or somewhere where there are other people, or knock on someone's door.

They should never play in dark or lonely places, or in empty streets or stairwells. They should stay with friends or in a group, and they shouldn't wander off on their own, even if they are playing Hide and Seek. Whenever possible, children should travel to school with a friend, and make it a rule that they let you know where they are going and what time they will be back.

Even the youngest child needs to learn their name, address and telephone number and, as they get older, their postcode. I can remember, as a Brownie, learning to use a public phone box, and it is something your children should be able to do. Explain how to make an emergency call and, if they don't have a phone card, how to reverse the charges so that they can contact you. If they get lost, the rule is to make their way to somewhere such as a shop where there are lots of other people and then ask for help. If they cannot find a shop assistant or a person in uniform in the shop, tell them they should ask for help from a man or woman who has children with them.

Teenagers coming home at night should either get lifts from parents or share a taxi. If they have to travel alone, they should get into a train carriage with other people and know what to do in an emergency if the train is cancelled or they miss it.

As a parent, you can be aware of the signs that something may not be right – if your child does not want to be with someone, find out why. A child that says 'please don't go out tonight' may in fact be saying 'please don't leave me alone with the babysitter'.

If you find that your child is being abused, try to stay calm and not to transmit your fears, anger, shock or embarrassment on to your child. Report the matter to the police and then channel your energies into assuring your child that *they* have done nothing wrong, that you are proud of them for coping and telling you what has happened, and that you love them. You may find that you need counselling help for both you and your child, especially if they get depressed; if so, talk to your GP about it.

Parents who drink too much

Having a parent who drinks to excess is another cause of depressed feelings in children and teenagers. Many feel that they themselves are the cause of their parents' problems and so have a very low opinion of themselves. It is hard enough for adults to cope when they have to live with an alcoholic, but for children it is like living on the edge of a precipice and not knowing what will happen next. Many children of alcoholics find that their childhood is snatched away from them. Instead of being cared for, they become the carers, particularly when it is the mother who drinks:

Philip's mother had been drinking heavily since she lost her job as a model and couldn't get any work again. His father knew there was a problem, but closed his eyes to it because he had his own life that he preferred to lead. For Philip, every day was a worry because he never knew what he would come home from school to. At 13 he should have been out with his friends or doing his own thing, but instead he would more likely have to get his drunk mother into bed. And as if this weren't bad enough, he had to clear up after her if she had been sick and listen to either a torrent of abuse, or her crying that her life was unfair, depending on how the alcohol affected her that day.

His attempts to hide bottles of wine and spirits so that she could not drink while he was at school seldom worked. If she didn't find the booze, she would buy more. In her more sober moments, she would tell Philip how sorry she was that he had had to get his own meals and wash his own clothes. She would talk about 'her little problem', by which she meant 'Mummy has a weak stomach'. Never would she admit to drinking or even discuss it.

Bearing the burden alone became too much for Philip. He tried talking to his father, but he got nowhere. He became so depressed that he started self-harming. His PE teacher noticed his hands and arms were constantly cut and bleeding, so took him to one side. After a lot of understanding and persuasion, he got Philip to tell him what was going on at home.

Philip's father was contacted, but was uncooperative. Two weeks later he packed his bags and left Philip and his mum to cope alone. It was at this point that Social Services became involved, and Philip got help from a school psychologist and his doctor to overcome the depression and self-harming.

He was also put in touch with Alateen, which is part of Al-Anon, which helps the family and friends of alcoholics and those with a drink problem. Alateen specifically helps those aged between 12 and 20 who are affected by someone else's problems with alcohol. Youngsters and adults alike can get help and support by telephoning the Al-Anon helpline on 020 7403 0888, or by visiting their website (www.hexnet.co.uk/alanon).

Parents who gamble

Being a child of a parent who gambles, whether it is on the horses or in another way, can cause the youngster to become depressed. It is hard for them to understand why Mum or Dad places a greater importance on gambling money away than paying the bills or providing food and a safe roof over their heads. The gambler always thinks that the big win is around the corner, but the child can only see lack of money and the bad moods his parent gets into when they lose.

Promises get made and broken, hopes are raised and dashed:

Megan desperately wanted to go on the school trip and her dad promised her that she would. When she asked for the deposit, he fobbed her off for two weeks saying 'wait until I get paid'. Payday came and went – and so did his money. Megan, used to this happening, couldn't bear the embarrassment of being made to look stupid at school, and told her French teacher that there was a family wedding at the time that the school trip was to take place and she wouldn't be able to go. The trip would have helped her with her French A level and, knowing this, Megan became very worried and depressed.

Keeping the family secret was difficult for her, especially as her father made out to family and friends that he was doing very nicely and he wouldn't admit that he had a problem. Resentment grew in Megan and so did her depression. Her mother, although worried about it, knew the reason, but was powerless to do anything about it.

Then, one day, the hire company repossessed the television and video recorder. Megan was incensed because she was recording educational programmes that went out during the night and that would help her with her A levels. To her mother's horror, she smashed up everything in her bedroom and was about to start on the living-room when her father came into the house. Instead, she rounded on him, struck him across the face, and then burst into uncontrollable sobbing. When her mother finally calmed her down she wouldn't speak, and didn't do so for the rest of that week. Instead she lay on her bed, staring into space.

Eventually her mother called the doctor who diagnosed severe anxiety and depression. When he asked her mother what had happened, everything about her husband's gambling came out. Eventually Megan recovered enough to take her A levels, but didn't get the grades to get into university. Instead, she took a job in a travel agency and hopes that when she feels completely better she will re-take her A levels.

Megan's father still gambles and refuses to accept that he has a problem. Megan and her mum sought help at the doctor's suggestion from Gamblers Anonymous. This excellent organization can be contacted on 020 7384 3040, or at their website (www.gamblers anonymous.co.uk). There is a section of this organization called GamAnon, which supports those living with a compulsive gambler.

Is your child scared?

Nightmares, claustrophobia, bed-wetting and phobias can all be caused by unhappy situations within a family. Once triggered, they can lead to depression.

Your home might be a happy one, but if it is not, and your child appears depressed or worried, then look carefully for the cause. Be honest with yourself. If you were a child living in your home, how would you be feeling?

When children have scared feelings, they need reassurance. Often they hear snippets of information, misinterpret them, and worry themselves sick. As parents we need to be aware of this and to be prepared to answer any questions that might be worrying our children. If your child is suffering from depression, get help from your doctor. Don't be ashamed or let your child feel this way. Tell them that sad feelings in your head can be helped to go away just as much as any other illness can be.

In a dangerous situation where violence or abuse is taking place, then make no excuses. Get your child out of that situation. Not easy, I know, but *essential* – even if it means hardship. No child deserves to be frightened or abused in any way.

Questions and answers

Q My seven-year-old daughter said something very strange to me last week. She told me that she didn't like being left in the house with my brother. When I asked her why, she said that she didn't know why, but said to 'forget it'. The thing is that I cannot. I asked my brother if he had done anything to upset her and he said that she was a 'spoilt brat who was out to cause trouble'. He refused to discuss it any more and stormed out. I am a single mum and my brother sometimes babysits when I have to work late. I feel very uneasy about this, but I don't know why.

A This statement came without prompting from your daughter and must be taken seriously. Something is bothering her and you need to know what it is, so talk to her again. Don't push her. Tell her that we all have people that make us feel uncomfortable, and ask her why she feels this way with her uncle. It could be that he is too strict with her when he is babysitting, doesn't pay her any attention, or it could be something more worrying. The fact that he wouldn't discuss it isn't a good sign. If you are feeling uneasy about things, then don't let him babysit again until you get to the bottom of this. If your daughter is unhappy being left with him, then he isn't the right babysitter for her anyway.

Q There are times when my husband's temper gets the better of him and he hits me. I know it is my own fault because I irritate him. He is always sorry afterwards and can be a kind man. My children have always known what has gone on, and when they know he is brewing they run upstairs and keep out of the way. My oldest son is 12 and came home from his Nan's to find me washing my mouth out because my husband had punched me in the face and my gums and lips were bleeding. He had a go at his dad, who gave him a really bad hiding. This was the first time that he had ever laid a finger on him. My son shut himself in his room and cried all evening. His father tried to talk to him and say he was sorry, but he wouldn't listen. Since then the atmosphere has been dreadful. My husband is like a volcano waiting to erupt and it is very scary. My son, on the other hand, has become moody and uncooperative and says he wants to go and live with his Nan. I feel caught in the middle.

A I understand how you feel, but you are the only person who can put things right. Your son is scared stiff to the extent of wanting to get away from home. Think about it. This isn't normal family life – it is a horrendous situation that cannot be allowed to continue. You live with a violent bully. Is this what you want for the rest of your children's lives and your own? Stop blaming yourself for being beaten, but you *will* be to blame if you stay with him and let your children get beaten. See a solicitor and speak to the domestic violence officer at your local police station. It is not an easy path to tread, I know, but it is the right one for you all.

7

Drugs, smoking, alcohol and self-harming

Drugs, smoking, alcohol and self-harming are things that youngsters turn to as a way of blocking out their depressed feelings when they cannot cope with their lives. The stories in this chapter are ones that I have collated over the years while being a guest speaker at world conferences on drugs and self-abuse. You may find these stories very upsetting as they are about young people who could not cope with their lives or their depressed feelings.

Let us first look at drugs, alcohol and smoking among those in their early teens from a survey carried out by the Department of Health, the Home Office and the United Kingdom Anti-Drugs Co-ordination Unit.

This survey was carried out among more than 9,000 secondary school children aged 11–15 in about 340 schools in England in the autumn of 1999. The main purpose was to give a comprehensive picture of drug use and to continue to monitor smoking and drinking among this age group.

Drug use among teenagers

Drug use among young people is one of the biggest concerns to us as parents, and it is worrying to note that the survey showed that more than 1 in 10 children aged 11–15 had used drugs in 1999. Cannabis was by far the most likely drug to have been used (11 per cent of pupils interviewed had used cannabis in 1999 but only 1 per cent had used crack or cocaine).

Trends in teenage drug use

The 1999 survey was the second one in which questions about drug use had been asked. There was no change between 1998 and 1999 in the proportion of 11–15-year-olds who had used drugs in the month before the survey: 7 per cent (about 1 in 14) had done so. However, there was a slight increase in pupils who used drugs in 1999 compared to 1998, but it was not statistically significant. The general picture is a fairly consistent one of small increases among both boys and girls, particularly those aged between 14 and 15.

The pattern of differences by sex and age was the same in 1999 as in 1998. Boys were a little more likely to have used drugs in the last year than were girls (13 per cent compared with 12 per cent), and for both sexes there were marked variations in relation to age (only 1 per cent of 11-year-olds had used drugs in the last year, but as many as 30 per cent of 15-year-olds had done so).

Regional and area variation in teenage drug use

The survey statistics showed that drug use among 11–15-year-olds appeared to be slightly more prevalent in the south of England than elsewhere, but differences were small. The proportion in each region that had used drugs in 1999 ranged only from 10 per cent to 14 per cent.

Drug use was significantly lower among pupils at schools in deprived areas than among those in non-deprived areas (10 per cent compared with 13 per cent). This is not perhaps what might be expected from the common belief that drug use is concentrated in poorer areas.

In the same way that drug use might be expected to be more prevalent in poor areas, it might also be thought that it would be more common in cities than in rural areas; however, the figures showed that pupils at schools in metropolitan areas were no more likely to be drug users that those in non-metropolitan areas.

The first occasion that drugs were used

An overwhelming majority of pupils (81 per cent) had used cannabis the first occasion that they had tried drugs, but 15 per cent had used glue and 10 per cent had used stimulants. Only 1 per cent had used opiates, and 2 per cent cocaine, on the first occasion.

Awareness and availability of drugs

About one-third (35 per cent) of pupils interviewed in the survey had been offered drugs, and the likelihood increased sharply with age (62 per cent of 15-year-olds compared with 13 per cent of 11-year-olds). All pupils were asked how easy or difficult it would be for them to get illegal drugs if they wanted to. As many as 43 per cent could not answer the question, probably because it had never occurred to them to try to get illegal drugs, but 29 per cent thought it would be difficult or impossible.

Smoking

According to the survey, the number of pupils who were regular smokers fell significantly during 1999, and this reduction appears to have occurred mainly in the 14- to 15-year-old age groups.

The government has set a target to reduce the number of children aged 11 to 15 who smoke regularly from a baseline of 13 per cent in 1996 to 9 per cent or less by 2010.

Although the proportion of pupils who are regular smokers (defined as usually smoking at least one cigarette a week) has fallen from 13 per cent in 1996 to 9 per cent in 1999, it *increased* to 10 per cent in 2000. However, because of the fluctuations in smoking behaviour since 1982, it is not possible to tell whether this is the beginning of a new upward trend in smoking.

As previous surveys have shown, girls are more likely to be regular smokers than boys (12 per cent compared with 9 per cent) and there is a sharp increase in prevalence with age (only 1 per cent of 11-year-olds smoke regularly, but almost one-quarter, i.e. 23 per cent of 15-year-olds, do).

The proportion of girls who smoke regularly has increased from 10 per cent in 1999 to 12 per cent in 2000, and the proportion of boys who smoke regularly has risen from 8 per cent to 9 per cent in the same period (although this latter change is not statistically significant).

Use of alcohol

The survey figures showed no change in the proportion of pupils who drank alcohol, although boys continued to be slightly more likely than girls to drink. The drinking behaviour of most children aged 11–15 is relatively modest, even among the oldest pupils. However, a small but significant proportion of those aged 15 (5 per cent of boys and 2 per cent of girls) said they drank almost every day.

The proportion of pupils who had had an alcoholic drink in the previous week rose steadily from 20 per cent in 1988 to 27 per cent in 1996. It then fell for the first time to 21 per cent in 1998 and 1999, and rose again to 24 per cent in 2000. This figure shows no clear pattern over time.

Both boys and girls were more likely to have drunk in the last week in 2000 than in 1999; and in 2000, boys continued to be slightly more likely than girls to have drunk alcohol in the last week (25 per cent compared with 23 per cent).

As with cigarette smoking, there seems to be a sharp increase in the prevalence of drinking with age: in 2000, 5 per cent of all pupils aged 11 had had a drink in the previous week, but 49 per cent of 15-year-olds had done so.

The average weekly consumption of alcohol among pupils who

drank in the last seven days has increased steadily from 5.3 units (equivalent to almost 3 pints of normal strength beer) in 1990 to 10.4 units in 2000.

Boys who drink tend to drink more alcohol on average over the course of a week than girls; boys drank an average of 11.7 units in 2000 compared with 9.1 units drunk by girls. For both boys and girls, the mean weekly alcohol consumption of those who drink is higher among older pupils.

These statistics are very worrying and are proof that we as parents need to keep an eye on our youngsters and watch for signs of drug, alcohol and cigarette use. The information I have given you is only a small part of a larger report, which can be accessed on the internet (www.statistics.gov.uk) for those parents who would like more details.

What can we do about the problem of drugs?

A few years ago I was invited to speak to the World Conference on Drug Abuse Prevention in Schools, which took place in Delhi. Here I met delegates from all over the world who were worried about the increased rate of trafficking, and in particular the number of children who were becoming addicts. I was horrified to learn that, in India, children as young as three and four were being introduced to drugs by the dealers, and there was a case where a teenager had sold one of his kidneys to get money to support his drug habit.

Since then I have spoken at many conferences in countries such as Nepal, Malaysia and the Philippines, and throughout Europe, and I am a member of the International Centre for Drug Abuse Prevention in Schools Executive Committee. I am not an expert on drugs, but what I do have experience of through my work as an agony aunt and counsellor is the emotional aspect of being a drug addict as well as the effect that it has on family and friends. There are many youngsters who grow up taking drugs because of peer pressure, convinced that they will not become addicted. However, a vast number *do* become addicted. Others turn to drugs because they cannot cope with the stress in their lives and become depressed. Some come from broken homes, others from stable family backgrounds, but each is using drugs as a prop to help them cope with their situation.

Peter has given me permission to tell his story:

Peter's father is a doctor who desperately wanted his son to follow in his footsteps. Having found A levels difficult, Peter was reluctant to go on to medical school, but because of pressure from his father he did. During his first year he was under such a strain that when a friend suggested drugs would help him to cope, he succumbed. As his addiction grew, his work became worse. He started to drink, then failed his exams and did not return to university for the second year. He stole money from his parents to support his addiction, and one night, in a fit of panic because he had not got a fix or any money, he broke into his father's surgery and stole drugs from there. When his father found out, he did not call the police because he couldn't face everyone finding out that his son was a drug addict, and for several weeks he supported his son's addiction.

Only when his mother, in sheer desperation, intervened and contacted the National Drug Line on her son's behalf did Peter start to get the help that he needed. He went into a Detox Centre and came off the drugs. The last time I heard from him he had a job as a driver and life was much better. He still got depressed at times because he felt he had failed his family, but was on antidepressants and was having counselling.

Drug addition is not something that happens only to other people's children. It can happen to ours. When it does, it sends the whole family into sheer desperation and panic. It can also (like Peter's father) cause embarrassment and shame.

This is sad, because our children are our future and we owe it to them to notice when they are under stress, that their behaviour has changed, or that something makes us think that they might be taking drugs. Whatever trouble our youngsters get into, they should never feel afraid to turn to us for help. There should be no blame, no recriminations on either side, just a coming together to work out the problems.

I received a letter from a lady who had seen from her window some children taking drugs in their garden. She wrote asking me whether or not she should say anything to the parents. The answer is a resounding YES ... because to say nothing could be to see a child die. The people who push drugs are making themselves rich at the expense of our children's lives, and it is up to us to make sure that this stops.

The symptoms of depression and those of drug abuse often go undetected by parents, and those that they do notice can get put down to teenage mood swings. Many people do not understand anything about drugs, so it is not surprising that it comes as a shock when they discover their child is taking them.

Drug abuse

Drugs are chemical substances that affect the ways that the body works. In the correct doses, drugs are used to cure diseases or ease symptoms, and come under the definition of 'medicines'. Not all drugs are medicines, though, and it may surprise you to learn that listed among 'socially and legally accepted drugs' are caffeine in tea, chocolate and coffee, nicotine in cigarettes, and alcohol – all things that most of us accept.

Drugs such as ecstasy, cocaine, cannabis and heroin are examples of drugs that are used for illegal social purposes. When these kinds of illegal drugs are used, they are likely to cause problems including mental illness, crime, violence and family breakdown.

A drug addict is someone who depends on a drug substance to feel well and able to cope with their life. Sadly, the drug may help in the beginning, but as time goes on the periods of depression and mental torture far outweigh the 'feel good' times.

Sniffing solvents and glue are also ways that young people get 'high', and sadly many have died through asphyxiation because of this. It is particularly important to be aware that younger children are very susceptible to glue sniffing.

Physical dependence is when a drug has temporarily or permanently changed a person's body or brain. When the drug is not available, the person suffers unpleasant withdrawal symptoms such as sickness, trembling and panic. Psychological dependence is more difficult to recognize, and occurs when a person feels emotionally disturbed without the drug, but does not show obvious symptoms.

These are some of the signs that a teenager might be taking an illegal drug:

- Unusual substances around the house – or discarded foil, silver paper or needles.
- Tubes of glue or solvent hidden in bedrooms.
- Tiredness.
- Bad temper.
- Unexplained anxiety and fear.
- Stealing.
- Furtiveness.
- Failing to do well at school.
- Lack of interest in things that were previously enjoyed.
- Crying, sadness and depression.

'Prevention is better than cure' is certainly true. A preventative home environment is one where children and parents talk about the risk of drug usage of all types, both legal and illegal. This way, the children gain a better understanding of the symptoms of depression and distress, so that when they get problems they feel that they can discuss them with their parents without shame, embarrassment or fear. This means they are less likely to turn to drugs or alcohol to try to cope with life, and also to notice when they are in danger of doing so.

Having said this, even the most caring and happiest of families can be faced with a drug abuse problem. If you think your child could be taking drugs, it is important not to rush in angrily as this will only make them clam up and withdraw. Ways of helping, once drug abuse is suspected or confirmed, have to be carefully planned. Reducing harm and increasing support in the least distressing way are the two main criteria.

Obviously you want to clamp down on drug abuse, but anger, blame, guilt or fear will only make things worse, further undermine your child's self-confidence, and make them feel even more depressed. Discovering what the underlying problem is – whether it be loneliness, bullying, being unable to cope with school, friendship or relationship problems – may not be easy, but being able to talk about these things will lift some of the pressure from your child.

Drug abuse should always be approached in a calm way, and it is vital to build up your child's self-esteem and self-confidence rather than becoming authoritarian and saying that they have to 'stop and behave themselves'. This won't work. Once you know your child is definitely using drugs, discuss with them ways of getting help. Explain to them that everyone has times when they feel depressed or cannot cope, and that they shouldn't feel ashamed about this. Seek help from their doctor and ask for details of counselling and drug advisory support within your area. A national organization called Turning Point (tel. 020 7702 2300) offers advice and gives details of local support groups.

Tell the school what is going on – don't feel it is something that has to be kept quiet. Most youngsters are first offered illegal drugs by friends at school, college or clubs. If your child is taking drugs, then there is a good chance that others are too, and their parents need to know.

Although drug abuse in the United Kingdom is a very serious problem, it is worth remembering that alcohol and cigarettes, although legal, cause far more damage to health than caused by all other forms of drug abuse combined.

Under-age drinking in teenagers is widespread, with many getting older friends to buy alcohol in supermarkets that is then consumed secretly. Sadly, some pubs also serve alcohol to young people who are under age. It is also about self-image, the feeling that it makes you appear more mature, and possibly sexually attractive. There is also the 'feel good' factor that consuming alcohol can bring about.

Anna's story encompasses all the abuses that are covered in this chapter. It is a harrowing story, but one that illustrates the depths of despair and depression that a young person can sink to:

Anna came to me for counselling when she was 18 because she was having flashbacks to when she took LSD.

Her life had been full of abuse and self-hate. She lived with her parents and two brothers, who were the source of most of her problems. Dad was a 'wheeler and dealer', dabbling in many things and earning a lot of money, although Anna told me that she didn't really know what he did. Appearances were most important for Anna's mother. Their house was the best kept in the road, but behind the door there were dark secrets.

When Anna was five, she saw her mother attack her father with a knife after a ferocious argument. This was the start of her nightmares when she would see hands with huge long fingernails made of blades coming towards her. She would wake up screaming, which annoyed her mother who hated being woken up. One night she got particularly angry with Anna and a row broke out between her and Anna's father. In the end the mother stormed off and slept in Anna's bed, telling Anna to sleep with her dad. It was then that the sexual abuse started. At five years old, Anna did not know what was worse – being alone with the nightmares or in bed with Dad. She only knew that she was scared – and that she felt unhappy and scared all the time. Her father told her it was their 'little secret' and that it was his special way of showing her that he loved her best. To counteract his guilt, he lavished gifts and money on her. Anna's mother became jealous and started to physically abuse Anna.

By the age of 12, Anna was smoking, drinking and sleeping around. At 14 she got involved with an 18-year-old friend of her brothers who introduced her to drugs. He then went to prison for drug dealing. By now, Anna's self-esteem was at an all-time low, her boyfriend was not around any more, her father was still sexually abusing her, and her mother was blaming her for everything and hitting her. It was at this point that Anna started self-harming and cutting herself. She told me that it helped with the pain she felt inside. She said she felt it was like being in a dark pit that she couldn't climb out of.

The pattern of drink, drugs, alcohol and self-harming continued until she was 16 when she met a man in his late twenties, who asked if she wanted to go out with him. That evening he took Anna to a local beauty spot where he played what she described as a 'death tape'. He gave Anna LSD, a hallucinogenic drug. It was the first time she had ever taken LSD and the trip she went on was horrific and psychologically disturbing. The guy soon realized what a bad state she was in, and drove her home and dumped her outside the house.

Anna's parents were out, but it took her brothers two hours to get her to walk through the door as all she could see were demons and snakes blocking her way. Her brothers never told her parents what had happened because the man in question was a friend of theirs. Anna was too scared and depressed to say anything either.

Three years later Anna was referred to me by her GP because she was still getting flashbacks to that night and was depressed. Although she was still on antidepressants, she had stopped hurting herself and taking illegal drugs. She still smoked and drank alcohol, but was trying to limit the amount. Throughout a year of counselling we managed to work through many of Anna's problems, and during this time she left home to live with her latest boyfriend, who was a nice chap, not involved in drugs, and really loved her.

Since then, he has asked her many times to marry him, but she has refused. Memories of her parents' violent marriage have made her scared to make this kind of commitment. She is also frightened that she would abuse any children she might have. For the time being she is content to leave things as they are. She is off the antidepressants now, but she still smokes and drinks – but to what extent is hard to tell.

Self-harming

Many youngsters, like Anna, turn to self-harm to overcome their depressed feelings. By cutting or injuring themselves they feel they are letting out the pain and anguish, and so get relief. Often they feel unloved or neglected.

Self-harming is probably one of the most misunderstood abuses, but it is one that sends out cries for help that can never be ignored.

I would like to end this chapter with a poem that was sent to me anonymously by someone who was self-harming. I think it sums up how desperate and depressed the teenager can become, often without their parents even realizing it. Be aware, it doesn't just happen to other people's children – it could happen to yours.

Pain

To bleed is to know you are alive
Even though inside you have died.
The pain of mutilation tells you
You live even when you feel dead

To know pain like we all do
is hard
To share pain is in vain,
To express pain I'm not sure
To release pain
Let the blood pour

Feel the scars you just made
Let the pain rush in,
As you touch them, press them, bleed them,
Is this life what I need or want,
Or is it all I know
The only way to show the pain
So deep inside.

8
Relationship problems

Relationships are important to us whatever our age, and when things go wrong it can be very distressing. Right from an early age children form friendships that are important to them. It is these friends who can make all the difference in going to school and being happy. In a good scenario, friendship is about warmth and caring, but when friends fall out it turns to unhappiness – and often depression. Feelings of being alone, rejected and not liked can turn an otherwise happy child into a desolate one.

Youngsters falling out with their friends

As we saw in Chapter 2, children can be very cruel, ganging up on each other and telling tales that are often not true. Every day countless primary school children come home from school in tears because they have fallen out with their friends. For a busy parent it may seem like a storm in a teacup, but to the child it is a major upset and one that needs a lot of understanding and comfort. They feel lonely, confused and hard done by. Some will be angry and want you to talk about it, others will keep quiet and bottle it all up. It is the ones who keep their worries to themselves who are more likely to get depressed, but the others can become victims as well.

It is important that you recognize any changes in your child right from playgroup age as it is never too early for a child to be hurt emotionally and to become sad and unhappy. Listen to what they say – have they stopped talking about a friend recently? Do they seem irritable, angry or stressed? In older children, have they stopped going out to meet their friends or no longer invite them home? Such problems happen to most children, and it is up to you to reassure them that even the best of friends fall out sometimes.

If you are concerned about a child who is at primary school, start by trying to get them to talk. Ask about their day, who they played with, or who they sat with at lunch. You will soon learn the areas of concern by what they are willing to talk about, and what they try to avoid. In most cases, children fall out one day and are friends the next. As they get older and are at secondary school, friendships become more intense, and there is likely to be a much longer and dramatic break-up period. This is probably because hormones are sloshing around and individual opinions are becoming much stronger. In these instances, encourage your teenagers to talk and to try to look at things from both sides. Explain that it is an important part of becoming mature to gain the ability to forgive and forget, despite whose fault it is.

One of my daughters fell out with her best friend over a meeting that never took place. Both said that they had turned up and waited half an hour (they had obviously waited at different places), and it ended up with her friend slamming the phone down. My daughter, now feeling she was the injured party, was quick to say, 'She is the one with the problem – and it is up to her to phone and say sorry.' When she had calmed down, I gently asked her how many friends she had that she could afford to lose one over this silly misunderstanding. After thinking about it, she replied 'not too many'. I asked her to think about how angry she was at waiting around and to try to understand that her friend had got equally fed up. This might also have been the last straw in a bad day for her friend, feeling she couldn't cope with any more.

After thinking about it, my daughter sent her friend a text simply saying 'Let's not fall out'. This opened the door to her friend texting back, 'Let's forget today and start again tomorrow'.

It could have gone on for days, and I know my daughter would have become increasingly miserable.

Problems between the sexes

Friendships may cause a lot of problems, but boyfriend and girlfriend relationships can bring even more. Below are some case histories that illustrate the problems that can occur and cause teenagers to become depressed:

Nadine and Terry were 14 when they first started seeing each other. Both sets of parents thought they were too young, but after many unsuccessful attempts to stop them seeing each other, they came to accept them as 'an item'. Problems started when they were 16 and Nadine did better in her GCSE exams than Terry did. Both went on to college, but Terry couldn't apply himself to the work like Nadine did. They began to argue. Terry said she was a 'swot and boring' – Nadine said that he wouldn't achieve anything in life unless he tried.

Often she would be doing homework while Terry went out with his mates. Gradually they grew apart, but neither of them wanted to hurt the other by ending the relationship. It was Nadine who wrote to me saying that she felt that Terry wasn't the right person for her. She felt pressurized into seeing him, and when she did they would end up arguing. Nadine was getting depressed and said that it was affecting her college work. It hadn't occurred to her that Terry wanted out of the relationship as well. I suggested that Terry wasn't happy either and that she should ask him how he felt about things. When she did, he told her that he still liked her a lot but he wanted to be with someone who wasn't studying all the time. Both of them were worried about what their parents would say, especially as it had taken them a long time to get used to them going out together. They need not have worried, because when they told their respective parents, they showed concern for both of them.

If your teenager is in a relationship that they don't want and are unhappy with, but don't know how to get out of it, suggest that they ask their boyfriend/girlfriend whether *they* are happy or not. In a lot of cases both partners feel stuck, but don't know what to do about it. It is important when they end a relationship to leave the other person with as much of their self-esteem intact as possible. To do this they have to emphasize that they are the ones who have changed towards the relationship, and not list a whole host of their partner's faults which they feel have caused the split:

Ian spent his last meeting with his girlfriend Holly justifying dumping her by telling her she was immature, selfish and brainless. He might have been right – but it left Holly depressed and on antidepressants for nearly a year, and she failed her A levels. He could have ended the relationship by telling Holly that he was feeling unsettled and wasn't ready for a steady relationship. She would have still been upset, but not annihilated by his thoughtless remarks.

If your teenager has been 'dumped', as they call it now, there is no point telling them that they will be better off without their girlfriend/ boyfriend. Even if they know this, they won't want you to tell them or have to admit it. Instead, let them know that you understand how hurt they feel and that you will be there to listen to them when they need to talk. Try to boost their confidence in any way that you can, because they will have taken a nasty knock.

Teenagers in violent relationships

Cindy, aged 19, lives at home with her parents and has severe depression. She is also in a violent relationship. Her parents are at their wits' end not knowing what to do for the best. They have spoken to solicitors, social workers and the police after Cindy has come home with a black eye or other injuries inflicted by Jaz, her boyfriend. Nothing can be done unless Cindy, who is an adult, makes a complaint about him. However, she won't because she believes that she loves him, insists that he does not mean to lose his temper, and believes him time after time when he says that he won't do it again – although he always does.

The number of girls and women, of all ages, who stay in violent relationships in the name of love is amazing. Cindy's parents believe she stays out of fear. Cindy won't accept this, or that her depression is anything to do with her relationship.

If you find your teenager being abused in a relationship, it is a worst nightmare come true. If, like Cindy, they are over 18, you can only support and advise them in as caring a way as possible. Violent people seldom change (and that includes women as well as men). Seeing their violent partner in their own secure environment often helps them see the truth. So when they feel as safe as possible, get them to invite their boyfriend/girlfriend to your home.

If they are under 18, it may be possible to keep them apart, but it is often very difficult. Remember, though, as a parent of a minor you have every right to protect them by seeking help from the police if you think that they are being abused.

Pressures to have sex

Although it is thought that most teenagers have sex, not all want to, or actually do so. This applies to boys as well as girls. Among those who claim to be having sex, there are many who are still virgins, but because of peer pressure the last thing that they want is for their friends to find out. An open exchange with your teenagers on sexual matters makes it easier for them to make decisions and to ask advice if they need to:

Paula was 15 when she started going out with Trevor, the son of her mum's best friend. To begin with they were both shy, and sex was not part of their relationship. Just after Paula's sixteenth birthday things went further, and they ended up having sex. For Trevor it was an amazing experience and one he wanted to repeat as often as possible, but Paula did not enjoy it, and found she was avoiding being alone with Trevor, or giving in simply to avoid an argument.

Their families had been friends for years and the parents trusted the youngsters, which made things worse for Paula because they would often be left alone. Although Paula still liked Trevor, she wished she had never given in and had sex. She wanted to end the relationship, but she couldn't because of the family friendship. Paula became withdrawn and depressed, often going to her bedroom straight from school and refusing to talk to anyone. Her mother was extremely worried, but could not get to the root of the problem. It was at this point that Paula wrote to me. She told me she felt trapped and that she never wanted to have sex with anyone ever again, saying 'it was horrid'. When I wrote back I told her that there was no reason why she couldn't stop seeing him. Relationships end every day and, at 16, no one could expect her to make a lifelong commitment to anyone. I also explained that many girls find their first sexual experience disappointing, but when they meet the right person they really enjoy it.

There was disappointment in both families when Paula split up with Trevor. Paula's mum had seen Trevor as a safe option for her daughter, rather than some of the other lads she might have chosen. Trevor's mum felt sore that her son had been rejected. Neither ever knew the real reason behind the split, and it was a shame that Paula felt unable to talk to her mum before she became so depressed. Once the depression had lifted, Paula soon became her old self again, but she told me in her last letter that it would be a long time before she would get involved with anyone else – the pressure had really scared her.

Difficulties concerning finding a partner

Thinking you are the only person without a boyfriend or girlfriend is really scary. Your friends seem so caught up in the excitement of having a relationship that they often have no time for you, which makes the disappointment doubly hard to cope with. You cannot force your teenagers into a relationship or find one for them. However, you can be aware that they feel lonely and unattractive to the opposite sex and may need their confidence boosted. If they confide in you, try to reassure them that there is someone out there for everyone, but sometimes it is worth waiting for the right person to come along.

Religious and racial pressures are the source of many of the letters that I receive from young people. There are parents who, although they have their best interests at heart, will not let their sons or daughters mix socially with their schoolfriends and only want them to be with people from their own religion or caste. Some insist that their children wear their national dress rather than school uniform, which makes them feel different from the others. Shanta, aged 13, wrote to me scared that her parents would find out that she had saved up for a mini skirt, like the other girls at school wore. She would leave the house in her Punjabi clothes, and change into her mini skirt in the public toilets. This was obviously a sad situation, but was resolved when compromises were reached after Shanta confided in her year head who liaised with her parents.

Some of the letters that I receive are from girls who are due to have an arranged marriage and yet they are seeing other boys behind their parents' backs. Others don't want to go ahead with the arranged marriage, especially if they are expected to marry someone much older or to go abroad to live. In cases like this, you have to see both sides. The parents, whose own marriages were arranged, see this as a natural and good process for their children. They are trying to shield them from harm by keeping them close to their own culture – no one could blame them for this.

For the youngsters, however, it is very difficult. They go to school or college and mix with students who can go out with whom they like, and who will make their own decisions in life. It must be a very confusing situation for them, especially as it is nobody's fault. Sometimes it helps to talk instead with someone who understands both the parents' and the youngster's point of view. The Asian Family Counselling Service is set up for this purpose. They offer advice to both parents and young people and can be contacted on 020 8571 3933.

Most of us will have been hurt at some time in our lives by a relationship. Whether it ended or hurt us another way, we know the anguish and pain that it can cause. The fall from happiness to depression happens so quickly that it is no wonder that relationships are a major cause of depression. Do not underestimate the strength of teenagers' feelings or dismiss them as being something that will pass. The heart knows no bounds when it comes to friendship and love, but when broken it can take a long time to mend.

Questions and answers

Q Everyone at college seems to have a boyfriend, other than me, so I lied and said that I had one as well. I gave them a name and made up a story about how we met. Because I live a long way from college I don't see friends from there over the weekends, so they wouldn't find out. It's my eighteenth birthday in three months and I would like to ask some friends to my party – but what do I do about the boyfriend I am supposed to have? Mum and Dad don't know that I have lied, and even if I say that we have split up, what if they mention it to my parents? I would die. The other problem is that there is a boy at college that I really like, but he thinks that I have a boyfriend as well.

A As soon as possible, get rid of this imaginary boyfriend and make room for a real one. Tell your mum that you got fed up being asked whether you had a boyfriend and that this is the only way you could think of to stop them going on at you. I don't think it will matter to your mum anyway. Relationships end all the time, and if you tell your friends now that it is over, then you will have plenty of time for this to settle and to work out how to get the boy you really like in time for your party.

Q I am a 17-year-old boy who has never had a girlfriend. Do you think there is something wrong with me? I look ordinary and I do most of the things other boys do, but none of the girls seem interested in me. Please can you tell me what I should do.

A I get letters like yours every week, and many of these are from people who are much older than you. Some boys get into casual relationships very easily, and seem to always have girlfriends, while others like you find it more difficult. You may think that there is no one interested in you, but I am sure there is. Maybe they are too shy to let you know. Have you asked anyone out yet? If not, give it a try. Make sure you have plenty of friends of both sexes and join as many clubs and activities as you can. The right girl hasn't come along yet but, believe me, she will. When she does, you won't have any more doubts about yourself.

Q Some of my friends at school say I am bossy and it gets them down. I think it is because I come up with ideas, and they don't. I am also an organized person, which is probably unusual for a 15-year-old boy. I like to know what I am doing and to be on time. My friends think I am trying to get into the teachers' good books. They are always late for lessons and never have the right books or equipment with them. I don't want my friends to be against me, but I cannot be like them.

A You don't have to change, but instead be a bit more aware that not everyone can be like you. Maybe your friends are not as quick off the mark as you are, so try to give them a bit more time to come up with some ideas, rather than always jumping in with your own. The chances are that they will still ask you what you think, but they won't feel that you are outshining them all the time. Ignore the remarks about you trying to get into your teachers' good books – you are there already, and if they cannot see that being on time for lessons and having the right equipment make sense, then that is their problem, not yours.

Q I have been seeing a boy on and off for a couple of months, but I have not told my mum. However, I left my diary around and Mum read it. Now she is acting very strangely towards me. If I try to talk to her about it, she says 'don't bother to share your secrets with me – it is too late now'. Before this, we always got on well. What can I do to make things right again? I didn't tell Mum because it wasn't serious and I was a bit embarrassed because it was my first boyfriend.

A I expect your mum is feeling hurt and upset about you keeping things from her for the first time, but I also think she feels guilty about reading your diary. Gradually the sarcastic remarks will cease, and when they do, try to mend the rift and tell her what you have told me. Give her some time and you will have the opportunity to sort this out.

Q I am ten and in the last year of primary school. There is a girl in my class that no one really likes and when my friends and I are talking, she pushes in and tries to be one of us. I thought I was the only one in my class who would be going to the church secondary school, but now she says that she is going. She will try to be my friend and I do not want that.

A It is nice to be one of a group, but it is awful when you are left on your own and she must be really unhappy. Can't you and your friends make an effort and include her for the last few months before you change schools? Maybe you will find out that she is not as bad as you think. You may also find that you are glad she is there when you go to your new school without your other friends. Try to be kind to her.

Q I had been going out with Nick for a year when we split up. We had got fed up with each other and agreed it was best not to go out any more. It has been six weeks now and I miss him a lot. I decided to telephone him to see if he was missing me. I got his mum on the phone as he was out, and she told me that he was going out with someone else, but she would tell him that I phoned. I don't think that she ever really liked me and seemed pleased to be able to tell me this. I haven't heard anything since, and I feel so miserable.

A It might be a good idea to phone again, or to write to him, as you only have his mum's word that he has met someone else, and you cannot be entirely sure that she gave him the message anyway. Sometimes the relationship needs some space. Lots of couples split up, the individuals go out with someone else, then get back together. So don't give up hope. At the same time, don't put your life on hold for him. Get out and have fun with your friends. If you are meant to be with him, things will sort out. If not, there will be someone else for you.

9

Do you understand your children?

If I asked you if you understood your children, I wonder how many of you could honestly answer yes. If I asked your offspring, especially the teenagers, the majority would say that you didn't. If you feel shocked by this, then don't be; think back to your own teenage years. Did you feel the same about your parents? Can you remember being exasperated over what you saw as their old-fashioned ways? They always seemed so opposed in the opinions they held. It is called the 'generation gap' and it is hard to remember the exact moment that we move across it. One moment you are a parent with the young child who hangs on to your every word, and the next you are in the unenviable position of still being a loving parent, but being seen as an obstacle to everything your son or daughter wants to do. Problems at home can lead to depressed feelings – and often without the parents realizing anything is wrong.

Let us take a look at the day-to-day problems that present themselves at home each day. To help you to do this, have a go at answering the questions below – whatever age your children are.

	YES	NO
1 Do you have 'house rules'?	❐	❐
2 If you have a partner, do you agree on these?	❐	❐
3 Are the children fully aware of these 'rules'?	❐	❐
4 Do they understand them?	❐	❐
5 Do they sometimes ignore them?	❐	❐
6 Do they ignore them all the time?	❐	❐
7 Do you expect reasonable behaviour from your child?	❐	❐
8 When they misbehave, do you reprimand them?	❐	❐
9 Do you feel that this is too much of an effort?	❐	❐
10 If you have a partner, do you agree on how to deal with bad behaviour?	❐	❐

DO YOU UNDERSTAND YOUR CHILDREN?

	YES	NO
11 Are your children rude to you?	☐	☐
12 Do they know that they can get away with bad behaviour because it is too much effort on your behalf to check it?	☐	☐
13 Do you spend time doing things with your child and give them periods of undivided attention?	☐	☐
14 Do you listen to them?	☐	☐
15 Do you say 'I am busy' when they want to talk to you?	☐	☐
16 Do they feel under pressure to achieve at school?	☐	☐
17 Are you competitive for your children?	☐	☐
18 Do they get on well with brothers and sisters?	☐	☐
19 Do you or your partner pay more attention to any one child than the others?	☐	☐
20 Are material possessions and designer labels very important to you and your children?	☐	☐
21 Are you so house proud that the children feel uncomfortable?	☐	☐
22 Is your home so untidy that the children are embarrassed by it?	☐	☐
23 Do you ever resent your children?	☐	☐
24 Do you sometimes feel that you love them, but you do not *like* them?	☐	☐
25 Do they live with arguments or fights in the home?	☐	☐
26 Do they feel secure and loved?	☐	☐

If you have teenagers, try answering the following questions too:

27 Do you argue with your teenagers all the time?	☐	☐
28 Do you get upset over their untidy bedrooms?	☐	☐
29 Do you try to choose their friends?	☐	☐

		YES	NO
30	Are you worried that they may be sexually active?	☐	☐
31	Do you suspect alcohol or drug abuse?	☐	☐
32	Are you allowing them any independence?	☐	☐
33	Do you worry about their safety?	☐	☐
34	Do they talk to you?	☐	☐
35	Would they come to you for advice?	☐	☐
36	Can you listen to them?	☐	☐
37	Can you see their point of view?	☐	☐
38	Privacy is important to teenagers – do they get this?	☐	☐
39	Are they coping with their school and exam pressure?	☐	☐
40	Do you still see them as your 'baby' and sometimes forget that they are growing up?	☐	☐
41	Do you expect too much of them?	☐	☐
42	Do they have girlfriend or boyfriend problems?	☐	☐
43	Do they have friends they invite home?	☐	☐
44	Are they lonely even though they have the family?	☐	☐
45	Do you ever tell them that you are proud of them and that you love them?	☐	☐

When you have answered these questions leave them for a while and then go back and read them again. You may find that the second time around your answers will change when you have had more time to think about things. It is often hard to admit to a problem at first, or even to recognize it. I have found in counselling that going through these problems with the teenagers afterwards is a real eye-opener for the parents. You may like to try this as a way of getting a better understanding between yourself and your teenagers and to see how they view the problems. It may also help you to reach compromises. It must not turn into an interrogation and you have to be prepared to listen to what they are saying. If you suspect your teenager is depressed, tread very carefully. It is probably best to put this exercise on hold until they have seen their doctor and are more able to cope with it. The last thing you want to do is make them feel threatened. Do not do this final exercise with younger children as they are not mature enough to understand your reasons for doing it and may feel very unhappy. The questions and answers, however, will give you an idea of the pitfalls that most families face and the need to listen to what your child is saying.

Noticing problems in children

Problems that arise with your children can usually be overcome once you recognize that there are difficulties. A change in behaviour will signify that something is amiss. Look for the following changes in them:

- Becoming quiet and withdrawn.
- Being unusually tearful.
- Not sleeping as well as they used to.
- Angry behaviour.
- Loss of interest in things that they normally enjoy.
- Frequent and unexplained tummy aches or feeling sick.

These are just a few signs and ones that should not be ignored. If you feel that there is a problem, your first instinct will probably be to ask them outright, 'What is wrong?' The direct approach does work with some children, especially the younger ones of around five to seven years of age, but not always. Most children, for whatever reason, hide their problems, almost to the extent of building a wall around themselves to try to block them out.

You know your own child, so you should recognize any behavioural changes. What you may not know is how best to find out what is upsetting them without making things worse. In my experience, worried or depressed children need to be surrounded by love and reassurance, and to have their parents' undivided attention and lots of cuddles. In their own time, they will talk about the things that worry them. Sometimes, like Kate below, it takes someone outside the family to see the problems before youngsters can talk to parents:

Kate at ten was what is termed a 'latchkey child'. Mum worked full time as a dental nurse; Kate's dad was a bus driver. On most school days, Kate would have to let herself into an empty house and wait for her mum to get in from work, which was an hour and a half later. The neighbour was always on hand in case there was a problem, and Kate could contact her mum on her mobile whenever she wanted. Going home was something that Kate dreaded. She was scared that one day someone would be waiting in the house and would hurt her. Some days she would hang around at the local shops or the library until it was nearly time for her mum to come home, rather than face being in the house on her own.

Not surprisingly, Kate became withdrawn and depressed. Often she would get angry towards her parents and would be told off for being rude. They knew there was a problem, but could not get her to tell them what it was. One day the next-door neighbour told Kate's mum that she had seen Kate waiting in the front garden in the rain. She thought that Kate had lost her key, and hurried out to invite her in. Kate looked flustered and quickly produced the key and went into the house. The neighbour told Kate's mum that it was not the first time that she had seen her behaving oddly.

The next day Kate's mum was at the school gates when Kate came out. The look of happiness on Kate's face brought tears to her eyes. Later that afternoon she cuddled her, and Kate, in between tears, told her how scared she was to be in the house on her own.

Kate's mum then told her employer that she would have to adjust her hours so that she could be home in time for her daughter each day. He understood, and although it meant a drop in her weekly earnings, Kate's mum knew that it was worth it.

Children who feel they are in the way

While most parents try to find time for their children, there are always those youngsters who feel they are in the way, and that it is easier to 'stay out of their parents' hair'. They feel they are to blame for everything that goes wrong:

Hayley's parents owned an antique shop and they lived above it. From an early age, Hayley could remember being told not to come into the shop, and to be careful not to touch anything as she passed through. She would be told to play in the back sitting room and wasn't to bother her parents while they were working.

It is not surprising that Hayley grew up feeling insecure and depressed. It appeared to her that a safer option was being not seen at all rather than run the risk of being shouted at. Eventually this extended into her school life, and beyond. She is still on antidepressants at 26 and scared to make ripples or complain about anything. She has never been confident in anything that she does. She hasn't had a relationship because of this, even though she desperately wants to be loved and to find someone that she can give love to as well. In her mind she is still the little girl who mustn't get in the way, and it will take a lot of counselling and encouragement to help her to overcome this.

Getting angry with children

Not all adult problems stem from childhood but, as you can see, some most certainly do. Like Hayley, most children hate being shouted at. They find it scary. When you shout at your child you cannot see the picture that you portray to them. No longer is there the kind Mum or Dad – all they see is a contorted, angry face, which frightens them. We have all screamed and shouted at our children, but next time you are tempted to do so, try to use a firm, controlled voice instead. Children respect boundaries and discipline, but they cannot cope with fear. I must mention at this point the effects on children when they hear their parents arguing and shouting. Once again, fear is involved and children cannot cope with too much of that. Try to remember when an argument breaks out that your voices will be raised and that little ears will be listening, probably at the top of the stairs where they may be crouched.

We all need to vent our anger at times, but try not to do it in front of the children or in their hearing, otherwise you may find you have a very disturbed child – like Peter, who is now ten, but his problems started when he was six:

Peter's parents were prone to arguing every weekend and he dreaded this. He endeavoured to please his parents, hoping that this would stop an argument breaking out. When the inevitable happened, Peter would think that it was his fault even though he had tried so hard to be good. He was too young to know or understand that his parents had argued from the day that they had met, and had always made up by the end of the weekend. All he could see was the weekend looming, with him waiting for the explosions of temper to happen. He became very aggressive at school, where he took his anger out on his classmates. By the age of nine Peter had to see a child psychologist because his behaviour had become so bad, both at school and at home. To begin with, the parents were present, but Peter clammed up and wouldn't say anything. Over the following months he saw the psychologist and had other counselling on his own. Gradually his fears were put into words. He felt that he was a bad person who made his parents unhappy, and that in turn made them angry. Things are better for Peter now, inasmuch as he has been reassured by his parents that he is in no way to blame. Sadly they still argue, though not so loudly. His parents, who say 'everyone argues, so it is not a problem', have turned down suggestions flat that they might benefit from counselling at Relate. I find that very sad.

Criticizing teenagers

'Why do they moan at me all the time?' is a constant cry that comes from teenagers every day. Well . . . why do we? I think that the main reason is that we find it hard to accept that they are moving from one phase of their lives to another. How many times have we told our children to 'grow up' or 'act your age and not your shoe size'? Yet when they put a foot forward towards making their own decisions and being independent, we quickly push them back in an attempt to keep control of the situation. Surely the easier option, rather than a constant battle, is to discuss moving certain boundaries, which gives some scope for individuality, and to keep others that maintain their safety and respect for other members of the family.

'Your room is like a tip' is something I read every week in letters from parents of teenagers. My answer to that is, 'So what!' If they want to live surrounded by squalor, then let them. Shut the door on the room and don't let it get to you. I decided years ago that an untidy bedroom was the least of my worries, compared to all the other teenage problems that could arise. So my sons' rooms resembled something like refuse tips, but at least they weren't taking drugs or in any trouble. I used to go in each day and open the window to let the fresh air in, put clean clothes on any clear space I could find, and give them clean sheets and towels every week (and insist that the dirty ones appeared in the washing basket that day). Occasionally I would suggest that they vacuum their rooms or hold an inquest into the shortage of mugs in the kitchen – which mysteriously always ended up in their rooms. After one such request, my youngest son produced 23 mugs from the bowels of his room – goodness knows how long they had been there! Apart from this, I never intruded on their privacy, or looked in the drawers, or got into a state over the mess. The interesting thing was, though, that my children (the boys, not the girls) may have had untidy bedrooms, but none of them ever made the rest of the house untidy. They knew that they had to respect our comfort as much as they wanted to do their own thing.

In the overall scheme of things, an untidy bedroom fades into obscurity – and so should what they wear. I say to all parents who object to their children's clothes and hairstyles, 'Bring out the photos of yourself as a teenager'. You will be horrified and stunned into silence – that is, if you can stop laughing!

So many teenagers become depressed through lack of understanding. They feel isolated by their parents, who seem to have suddenly become very dictatorial. It is not easy to bridge the generation gap between teenagers and parents. The parents have often forgotten what it was like to be a teenager and the hassles they may have had with their parents. The teenagers, on the other hand, are under the misapprehension that we were born middle-aged, and we couldn't possibly understand how they are feeling. The truth is that the problems facing teenagers today, apart from drugs, are more or less the same as they were when we were young. Relationships, friends, curfews, feeling you don't fit in, being treated as a child, not allowed to stay up for half the night, and sex. Teenagers seem to think that they have the monopoly on sex, and cannot believe that their parents ever felt sexy or faced the same temptations as they do. The fact that they were produced through sex is something that they hastily skate over and choose to forget!

Getting the balance right

As parents, it is difficult to let go. We worry, and rightly so, as our parents did before us. The vital thing is to get the balance right. Don't argue about things that really don't matter. Try to let them make some decisions themselves, but explain that you have to be responsible for their safety. Teenagers will often ask questions at a time when it is difficult to stop and talk. Try not to say, 'Don't bother me now.' Instead say, 'I want to discuss this with you, but it is difficult at the moment. Let's talk when I have done this, or after supper.' You must remember that they may have been plucking up courage to ask about something for ages, and you do not want to miss the opportunity to talk. It may never come again.

There will be times when your children may find you embarrassing or you fall out over their friends. You cannot change yourself to fit in with the role your teenagers want for you, no more than you can expect to choose their friends. But discussing differences of opinion will give a better understanding between you and your teenagers, and you will have to find time to do this. Whenever possible, sit down at the table to eat meals as a family. This promotes conversation and a better understanding for everyone about other members of the family. Some parents have a 'family session' with their teenagers each week or month where problems are discussed and compromises reached. It is a good idea, although it can take time to establish and work to its best effect.

Questions and answers

Here are some problems that arise between parents and children:

Q When I was 11 I was attacked and sexually assaulted. This has always made me worried about my daughter. The problem is that it has become such a worry that I cannot bear for her to go out anywhere on her own. She never goes out in the evenings or at the weekends; I invite her friends to our house rather than her going out. When I think what may happen, I just cannot let her go. Although my husband understands the problems, he says that I cannot wrap her up in cotton wool for the rest of her life. She is 15 and he says that she should be allowed to go out with her friends. What do you think?

A Having had a similar experience myself when I was a child, I know exactly where you are coming from, but I agree with your husband that you cannot go on transferring your fears on to your daughter because that is not fair. You should let her go out. You *will* worry, just as any other mother, maybe a lot more, but you cannot watch over her for ever and make her different from everyone else. She needs to become 'streetwise', and you need to relax and maybe get counselling to help you overcome the fears of what happened to you all those years ago.

Q I am 13 and I want to go to a party next week. My parents say that I can go, but they won't allow me to stay after midnight and they insist on picking me up after the party. If I were a girl, I would

understand, but surely a boy should be allowed to stay up and not be
picked up by his parents.

A   Think yourself lucky – most 13-year-olds wouldn't be able to stay
out that late anyway. Yes, girls may be more vulnerable sometimes,
but boys are not excluded from being victims of violence late at night.
If I were you, I would stop moaning; otherwise your parents may
change their minds and not allow you to go at all.

Q   My daughter Nicky is 14 and will not get out of bed in the
mornings. I have to call her several times, and usually end up having
to drive her the two blocks to school, which she is quite capable of
walking, so that she is not late. The other problem is that she doesn't
do her homework, but expects me to sign the homework book to say
that she has. She seems to do the opposite to whatever I say. Now I
have had a letter from the school asking why she has not handed in
work that I say that she has done. What should I do?

A   It sounds as if your daughter has got you dangling on a piece of
string, and it is time to give her a shock. Stop waking her up and let
her be late. Refuse to give her lifts or sign her homework book any
more, unless she does the work. I suggest you speak to her form
teacher, or head of year, and explain what you intend to do. Discuss
how she behaves at school. While she thinks you are always going to
bail her out, she won't learn to take any responsibility for herself.

Q   I am 16 and have a mother who is dead embarrassing. She is 54
and dresses loud. She buys all her clothes from charity shops even
though she can afford to shop anywhere. Her clothes are always
brightly coloured, flowery and eccentric. My dad thinks that she is
wonderful, but I think she is crazy because she says and does the most
outlandish things. For example, she refused to talk to anyone, other
than in French, for a whole week. She only knew a few phrases that
she had learnt that week at evening classes. The rest of the time she
used a book, and we had to wait while she looked things up. She
wouldn't let us eat until we had said thank you in French. Dad thought
that it was great and encouraged her. I went to the supermarket with
her, thinking she would talk in English, but she spoke to the two
assistants in French, who did not understand a word she had said.
Another time, she sang a song on a bus. She says 'buses are so
dreadful that they need cheering up'. Some of the other passengers
joined in – it was awful. My friends think that she is smashing, but I
dread to think what she will get up to next.

A   Do you know, there are thousands of deadly dull and boring people around and the world needs colourful people like your mum. At 16, I do understand that you would prefer a mum who fades into the background and was always there for you, but who didn't stand out too much. Believe me, as you get older, you will be glad she is like this because life will never be dull while she is around. Your dad is proud of her, and you should be as well.

Q My parents have 'grounded' me because they have found out that I have been going to a pub. I think it is unfair because all my friends go and their parents don't kick up a fuss. We only have a couple of beers, and we drink beer anyway when we are at each other's houses (except when at our house, because my parents won't allow it). My friends' parents buy the beers from a supermarket each week. We see it as part of becoming mature. Why are my parents such a drag?

A They probably seem like a drag to you because they have to be firm in order to keep you in line. You shouldn't be drinking in a pub at 15 and the landlord should not be serving you because it is illegal. You say that your friends' parents don't make a fuss, but then maybe they do not care about their sons as much as your parents do. Buying beer and encouraging youngsters to drink on a regular basis is not what responsible parents do, and if that's what they want for their children, just be grateful that yours want something better. The occasional drink at home isn't wrong, but you have to drink in moderation. Always remember that people who have to drink to be mature have a very wrong outlook on life.

Q My daughter is going around with a girl who I don't think is right for her. She has always been a quiet girl, very nice natured and easily taken advantage of. This other girl comes from a broken home, and one of her brothers – who lives with his dad (this girl lives with her mum) – has been in trouble with the police for stealing a car when joyriding. I told my daughter that I didn't want her going around with this girl any more, and she said that I was being unfair to her friend who hadn't done anything wrong.

A Try to meet the girl and judge her on her own merits rather than on the gossip that you have heard about her family. You cannot choose your daughter's friends, and it sounds as if this girl really needs a nice friend like your daughter.

10

Afterword: the challenge of bringing up our children

Dear Friend,

The job of bringing up children is one of the most rewarding but difficult tasks that anyone can take on. This is a skill that you haven't been trained in. There are no holidays as such and no wages at the end of the week. Someone once said to me, 'Children bring a lot of joy, and a lot of tears' – and that's true. Sometimes it seems that the joy has disappeared, but it is always there if you look for it.

When the going gets tough, look around, and you will see other parents who are muddling along just as much as you are. None have all the answers, but all have one thing in common – they are entrusted with young lives. Most won't have a clue about child rearing when their babies are born, but they learn as they go (even from their mistakes). There is no such thing as 'perfect parents' – they don't exist. Instead, there are 'good parents', who do their best in every way that they can.

Sadly, communication does break down at times. Problems go unnoticed by even the most caring of parents. The warning signs that a child or teenager has become depressed are one of them. Be aware, depression does not only affect adults or other people's children. It doesn't signify a weakness, nor is it something to be hidden or ashamed of.

If you have the slightest inkling that your child is depressed, do something about it now. Get help from professionals, family and friends. Let your child know that they have nothing to feel ashamed of, and that they are surrounded by those who love and care for them.

If they need medication, discuss any concerns with their doctor. Answer your child's questions as honestly and caringly as you can. Never let them feel that they have failed you or themselves. Depression is an illness, just like any other, and together you can help it to pass.

We have travelled a long way together through this book and probably touched upon many raw nerves. Maybe it has helped you to see where the problem areas arc for you and your children, or enabled you to realize that you are not doing so badly after all.

I was sent the following few words by Jason, a 13-year-old teenager who was depressed because his parents kept arguing and had no time for him. He told me that this was how he felt:

'I am sinking, down, down, down – into the dark pit below me'

I shuddered as I read these words. I could almost feel myself sinking down with him. For a 13-year-old boy to feel such depths of despair is a dreadful thing. His parents were oblivious to his feelings because they were so caught up in their own problems. To them, he had become a moody teenager – the fact that he might be depressed wasn't even considered.

It was his form teacher who contacted Jason's parents. She had experience of other children who had been depressed, but she was met by a wall of anger from his parents who saw depression as a stigma that was certainly not going to be attached to their son! Eventually they were forced to face up to the fact that their son was undoubtedly depressed when he took an overdose. Jason was admitted to hospital and saw a counsellor before he was discharged. Over the coming months he was treated for his depression and his parents tried not to argue. Because of their mutual concern for Jason, it brought about a better understanding between them, and they decided to go to Relate for counselling. The following Christmas I received a card from Jason, and along with the usual festive message he had written:

'I feel like a bird who has been let out of a cage –
I am flying high, Vicky'

I can't tell you how much it meant to read these words and to know that he was on the mend.

I wonder if any of you have come across the writings of Kahlil Gibran and his book *The Prophet*. Born in 1883 in Lebanon, this poet, philosopher and artist expresses his thoughts on life. They are simple, yet so poignant. About children he says:

You may give them love, but not your thoughts,
You may have their bodies, but not their souls,
For they dwell in the House of Tomorrow
Which you cannot visit not even in your dreams.

You are the bow
From which your children as living arrows
Are sent forth.
The Archer sees the mark upon the path of the infinite
And he bends you with his might
That his arrows may go swift and far.

What a wonderful way to describe the lives of the children we bring into the world. We can guide our children's lives and watch over them so that they don't become depressed. By doing this, we can look back in years to come and know that we have done our best.

Take care.

Kind regards,
Vicky

Sources of help

Al-Anon
Tel: 020 7403 0888 (helpline)
Website: www.hexnet.co.uk/alanon

Alateen (Alateen is part of Al-Anon, and specifically helps those aged
   between 12 and 20 who are affected by problem drinkers)
Website: www.hexnet.co.uk/alanon/alateen

Asian Family Counselling Service
Tel: 020 8571 3933

Childline
Tel: 0800 1111 (24-hour free helpline)

Depression Alliance
35 Westminster Bridge Road
London SE1 7JB
Tel: 020 7633 0557
E-mail: information@depressionalliance.org
Website: www.depressionalliance.org

Eating Disorders Association
103 Prince of Wales Road
Norwich NR1 1DW
Tel: 01603 621 414 (helpline) (open 9 a.m.–6.30 p.m. weekdays)
Tel: 01603 765 050 (youth line for under-18s) (open 4 p.m.–6 p.m.
   weekdays)
Website: www.edauk.com

Gamblers Anonymous
Tel: 020 7384 3040
Website: www.gamblersanonymous.co.uk

Home Education Advisory Service
PO Box 98
Welwyn Garden City
Herts AL8 6AN

Kidscape
2 Grosvenor Gardens
London SW1W 0DH
Tel: 020 7730 3300 or 08451 205204 (local rate)
Website: www.kidscape.org.uk

NSPCC
Tel: 0800 800 500 (24-hour free helpline)

ParentlinePlus
Tel: 0808 800 2222 (helpline)
Website: www.parentlineplus.co.uk

Samaritans
Tel: 08457 90 90 90 (24-hour free helpline)

Stepfamily Scotland
Tel: 0131 225 5800
Website: www.stepfamilyscotland.org.uk

Turning Point
Tel: 020 7702 2300 (Turning Point offers help with drug abuse)

Index